GIVE US

★★★ THE ★★★

VOTE!

OVER 200 YEARS OF FIGHTING FOR THE BALLOT

SUSAN GOLDMAN RUBIN

HOLIDAY HOUSE • NEW YORK

To Andrew A. Rubin, with gratitude

HOLIDAY HOUSE is registered in the U.S. Patent and Trademark Office.
Printed and bound in September 2019 at Toppan Leefung, DongGuan City, China
www.holidayhouse.com
First Edition
1 3 5 7 9 10 8 6 4 2

Library of Congress Cataloging-in-Publication Data
Names: Rubin, Susan Goldman author.
Title: Give us the vote : over two hundred years of fighting
for the ballot / [Susan Goldman Rubin].
Description: First Edition. | New York : Holiday House, [2019] | Audience:
Ages: 10–18. | Audience: Grades: 7 to 8. | Includes bibliographical references.
Identifiers: LCCN 2019007647 | ISBN 9780823439577 (Hardcover)
Subjects: LCSH: Voting—United States—History—Juvenile literature.
Political participation—United States—History—Juvenile literature.
Elections—United States—History—Juvenile literature.
Elections—Corrupt practices--United States—History. | Democracy—United
States—History—Juvenile literature. | United States—Politics and
government. | United States—Race relations—Political aspects.
Classification: LCC JK1978 .R83 2019 | DDC 324.6/20973—dc23
LC record available at https://lccn.loc.gov/2019007647

CONTENTS

"The right to vote is precious and almost sacred."

—John Lewis, civil rights leader and congressman

PROLOGUE

"North Dakota's voter ID law aimed to silence Native American voters."

—Jamie Azure, (1977–), Tribal Chairman for the
Turtle Mountain Band of Chippewa Indians

AS A BOY, JAMIE AZURE, NOW THE TRIBAL CHAIRMAN FOR THE Turtle Mountain Band of Chippewa Indians, hiked to the post office to pick up his family's mail. "We didn't have an official street address," he said. "Nobody did. . . . Most streets don't have signs." But a law in North Dakota that went into effect before the 2018 election required voters to present IDs with street addresses at the polls. Members of tribes like Jamie's, living on reservations in rural areas, did not have street addresses or numbered roads. They only had post office boxes, and those didn't qualify.

"This [law] was clearly designed to target Native Americans," said Azure. "We used to be able to cast ballots in state, federal, and tribal elections without an ID if we signed an affidavit or a poll worker vouched for us."

The law, passed by the Republican-controlled legislature, could have prevented thousands of Native Americans from voting. The Turtle Mountain Chippewa tribe responded by suing the state of North Dakota over voter ID requirements. However, an appellate court ruled against the tribe, and in October 2018 the U.S. Supreme Court upheld the ruling.

"This is our territory, this is our land," declared Judith LeBlanc of the Caddo Nation. "For them to say that we need to have an address in order to vote is an insult."

The Spirit Lake Sioux tribe sprang into action by filing another lawsuit against the state of North Dakota. The suit claimed that the law was unconstitutional. It violated section 2 of the Voting Rights Act (VRA) of 1965, which prohibited voting procedures that discriminate on the basis of race.

Before the passage of the VRA, most Native Americans didn't have the right to vote. Native Americans were not granted full citizenship until 1924 when Congress passed the Snyder Act. Even then, the right to vote was granted state by state. It wasn't until 1962 that Native Americans gained voting rights in all the states. Even then, many states continued to make it difficult for Native Americans to exercise their rights. The VRA was meant to ensure that right to vote.

But the new law in North Dakota barred many Native Americans from the polls. The Spirit Lake Sioux lawsuit requested that the law be suspended in time for the midterm election. The request was denied by the U.S. district court.

Indigenous people fought back. A Native American voting rights group called Four Directions developed a system that allowed tribe members to point to residences on electronic maps and generate addresses. Tribal officials then printed IDs that the voters could use to cast ballots.

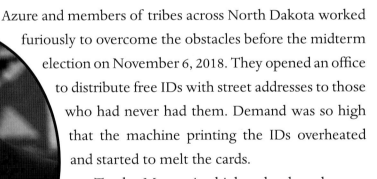

Jamie Azure, Tribal Chairman, Turtle Mountain Band of Chippewa.

Azure and members of tribes across North Dakota worked furiously to overcome the obstacles before the midterm election on November 6, 2018. They opened an office to distribute free IDs with street addresses to those who had never had them. Demand was so high that the machine printing the IDs overheated and started to melt the cards.

Turtle Mountain high school and community college students helped lead get-out-the-vote efforts on the reservation. A nonpartisan rally starring singer Billy Ray Cyrus drew a crowd of fourteen hundred. On Election Day, students walked out of class and marched to a polling site on their reservation. They carried signs that read DON'T DISENFRANCHISE US and WE ARE THE GRANDCHILDREN OF THOSE YOU COULDN'T REMOVE.

WHAT INSPIRES YOU?

Jamie Azure speaks at a get-out-the-vote rally at Belcourt Community College, North Dakota, October 2018.

At Standing Rock Sioux Reservation, volunteers knocked on doors, helping residents file absentee ballots. Young people decorated a Get Out the Vote bus that drove from community to community on the reservation, which covers just over thirty-five hundred square miles, taking eligible voters to the polls. Banners proclaimed STANDING ROCK WILL VOTE.

And it did. Local precincts reported a record turnout in North Dakota's counties with large Native American populations.

Alexis Davis, a member of the Turtle Mountain youth council, said she wasn't that interested in politics before this election. "But then this voter ID law came," she said, "and then I was paying attention. They were trying to take a right away from us. It made us want to go in there and vote twice as much and make a statement."

CHAPTER 1: THE POWER OF THE BALLOT

"If you can't vote then you're not free; and if you ain't free, children, then you're a slave."

—Hosea Williams (1926–2000), civil rights leader

AS AMERICAN CITIZENS, BLACK PEOPLE GAINED THE LEGAL right to vote when the Fifteenth Amendment to the Constitution was ratified in 1870. In much of the South, however, white politicians, enforcement agents, and civil servants blocked attempts by black people to register to vote through racist laws, intimidation, and discriminatory tests. In Alabama, for instance, black people trying to register had to pass literacy tests white people did not have to take that required them to explain excerpts of the Constitution and name all sixty-seven county judges in the state. Registrars even used trick questions on these tests, such as asking the number of feathers on a chicken or the number of jelly beans in a gallon jar. Some states and communities imposed a poll tax that most black people couldn't afford to pay. Many white Southerners were afraid that if black people could elect officials, whites would lose their political dominance and their power over blacks.

Fannie Lou Hamer, the granddaughter of enslaved people, didn't learn that she had the right to vote until 1962, when she was forty-four. Mrs. Hamer, a poor sharecropper, attended a civil rights meeting in Sunflower County, Mississippi, and heard that she had a chance to vote out "hateful policemen" who terrorized her community. Attempting to register to vote resulted in her being ordered off the plantation that was her home. Even worse, she was jailed and beaten, and her life was threatened. "Well, killing or no killing," said Mrs. Hamer, "I'm going to stick with civil rights." Her spirit and singing inspired people, and the Student Nonviolent Coordinating Committee (SNCC) recruited her to be a leader in the civil rights movement. "I am determined to get every Negro in the state of Mississippi registered," she said.

In 1963 more than half the population of Selma was black. Yet not one black person had registered to vote in sixty-five years. Black adults hesitated to protest. They feared losing their jobs and their homes, like Mrs. Hamer, and even their lives.

That year, civil rights leader Dr. Martin Luther King Jr. started a campaign in Birmingham, Alabama, to urge black people to register to vote. Dr. King asked Reverend James Bevel to help him.

Reverend Bevel had the idea of enlisting middle school and high school students in the campaign. He recruited young people to join the movement and participate in a "Children's Crusade" to attract national attention. On May 2, 1963, as the first big event of the effort, the young people marched from the 16th Street Baptist Church to downtown Birmingham. Police arrested the children and carried them off to jail. The next day hundreds more youths gathered to march and were attacked by police officers and police dogs. Images of the violence outraged people across the country.

"Students did not have as much to lose as their parents," said Jeremiah Hunter, who was a junior at E. M. Brown High School in Birmingham. "Although I did not have permission to leave school, I felt strongly about participating, so I skipped school."

"Most of us were not old enough to vote, but we were determined to fight for the right of our parents to vote," said Charles Bonner, a student at Hudson High School in Selma. "If we won, we would have that right when we became adults. We learned that the power of change was in the power of the ballot."

"The right to vote was a lifelong dream of many adults in my family and the community," said Paulette Patterson Dilworth of Selma, Alabama.

Reverend Bevel held mass meetings at the 16th Street Baptist Church to train students. "We were taught the nonviolent way," recalled Carrie Manuel-Prowell. Dr. King's aide, Hosea Williams, led meetings too. Williams explained to the kids that the right to vote meant freedom to elect local sheriffs, judges, and mayors, as well as state governors and even the president!

Brave children kept marching and getting arrested until a tentative agreement

A minister conducts a mass meeting in a Selma church to raise spirits and recruit participants for Student Nonviolent Coordinating Committee (SNCC) voter registration.

was reached on May 9 between the black community and city officials to desegregate local businesses and free the students. Young people continued to be active in the movement.

"I was eight years old when my grandmother took us to our first mass meeting," recalled Joanne Bland. "We started singing about freedom and hope and things started coming together."

In December 1963 Dr. King met with President Lyndon B. Johnson at the White House. He asked the president to present a voting rights bill to Congress that would guarantee black people the right to vote, their birthright as Americans. Johnson said, "I'm going to do it eventually, but I can't get voting rights through in this session of Congress."

In 1965 Dr. King returned to Selma to kick off a civil rights campaign. On January 2, the anniversary of the signing of the Emancipation Proclamation that freed most enslaved people in the United States, he delivered a speech at Brown Chapel African Methodist Episcopal Church. "We must be ready to march," he told the crowd. "We must be willing to go to jail by the thousands."

"Don't worry about your children," he reassured parents. "Don't hold them back if they want to go to jail. They are doing a job for not only themselves but for all of America and for all mankind."

On January 18, King's Southern Christian Leadership Conference teamed up with SNCC leaders for a protest march to the Dallas County Courthouse in Selma. Sheriff Jim Clark was waiting for them. Clark, an avid segregationist, wore a pin printed with the word NEVER, his response to the civil rights anthem "We shall overcome."

"Negroes will never overcome us," he told newsmen.

Tena Lundy Moten, a fifth-grader at Payne Elementary School, cut class to join the protest. "Although I was only ten, I was given a sign to hold while we marched to the courthouse for the right to vote," she recalled. "The police and sheriff would be there with their billy clubs, threatening to beat us if we did not disperse and return where we came from, and saying, 'No niggers are going to vote here.'"

Clark herded four hundred prospective voters into an area behind the courthouse and made them stand there for hours before sending them home. Photographers from the *New York Times* and the *Washington Post* snapped

Police officer taking signs from adolescent civil rights demonstrators who had been marching down a sidewalk during the Children's Crusade in Birmingham, Alabama, May 3, 1963.

pictures of Sheriff Clark yanking Amelia Boynton, a voting rights leader, by the collar and violently shoving her into a squad car. The photos appeared on the front pages of the newspapers and on TV. People were appalled by Clark's rough treatment.

On Monday, February 1, one of only two days of the month that the registrar's office was open, Dr. King led a march to the courthouse. But the Selma police stopped the marchers because they didn't have a parade permit. Dr. King said, "I gotta keep on." So he and five hundred young people were arrested and thrown into jail. "There are more Negroes in jail with me than there are on the voting rolls," wrote Dr. King.

"When we filled the city and county jails," said Charles Bonner, "we were placed in Camp Selma, a work camp for state inmates. The conditions were horrible. Nearly sixty girls occupied one cell with access to one toilet."

"I spent eight days in a jail cell with thirty-six other schoolmates," recalled

Police dog attacking Walter Gadsden, a student at Parker High School, during a civil rights demonstration in downtown Birmingham, Alabama, May 1963.

Bessie Houser Hunter. "The condition of the cell was horrifying: two cots without linen, battered filthy mattresses, a dirty and rusty sink with a dripping faucet of only cold water, a commode next to the sink that was stopped up from overuse, a half roll of toilet paper that disappeared rapidly. They served small portions of unseasoned black-eyed peas two times a day. The cell was smothering hot during the day, and very cold at night as we slept on the dirty concrete floor."

"We took turns sleeping," said Helen Brooks, "and sang all night to keep the jailers awake."

"Two months before my fifteenth birthday, I marched for voting rights," said Denise Jarnigan-Holt. "I was jailed for weeks at a time. . . . When I went to jail the first time, the guard that checked me in with fingerprints said to me: 'Go home. You shouldn't be here. This is going to go on your record and will follow you for the rest of your life.' I said to him, 'If I don't stand up for my rights today, that will follow me for the rest of my life.'"

On Monday, February 15, the second day the registrar's office was open, marchers made another attempt to register. Sheyann Webb had started attending meetings at church when she was eight years old. Her parents "hadn't even tried to register because they knew they didn't have a chance." But inspired by Sheyann, and as a gift to her for her ninth birthday on February 17, they joined the rally. By late afternoon they entered the courthouse and were told they couldn't be registered that day. They were given a number to "hold" their place till the next registration day. Mrs. Webb was now determined.

"As we hurried home Momma was saying she didn't care how long it took," recalled Sheyann. "She was going to be back each day they held registration until she could vote."

CHAPTER 2: WALK FOR FREEDOM

"Give us the ballot! We are *demanding* the ballot."

—Dr. Martin Luther King Jr. (1929–1968),
civil rights leader and Nobel Peace Prize laureate

THE EFFORTS IN SELMA INSPIRED BLACK CITIZENS IN neighboring counties to fight for the right to vote. On February 18, 1965, there was a nighttime demonstration in Marion, the seat of Perry County, Alabama. State troopers attacked the protesters with nightsticks. Jimmie Lee Jackson,

Singing freedom songs under police guard, hundreds of schoolchildren march down the middle of the street toward a detention compound after their mass arrest on February 3, 1965, in front of the Dallas County Courthouse in Selma, Alabama.

Police officers arresting Mattie Howard during the Children's Crusade in Birmingham, Alabama, May 8, 1963.

who had unsuccessfully tried five times to register to vote, hid in a café with his mother and grandfather. Ten state troopers rushed into the café and beat Jackson's mother. He rushed to protect her and a trooper shot him in the stomach. A week later Jimmie Lee died. At his funeral service Dr. King said, "Jimmie Jackson just wanted to vote. Now we must see that Jimmie Jackson didn't die in vain."

Reverend James Bevel suggested marching from Selma to Montgomery, the state capital, to protest Jackson's death and demand the right to vote. Dr. King had doubts because of the potential danger to participants. But John Lewis, SNCC's chairman, insisted on marching. On the morning of Sunday, March 7, Lewis and Hosea Williams led six hundred residents of Selma from Brown Chapel in a "Walk for Freedom" to Montgomery.

As the marchers crossed the Edmund Pettus Bridge, they faced Alabama state troopers and Sheriff Clark's posse carrying bullwhips and batons wrapped in barbed wire.

"The police were on horses chasing us," recalled Tena Lundy Moten, a fifth-grader. "I ran as fast as I could, but I could not outrun police on horseback. A policeman pressed a stick in my side that felt like electricity going through my body."

"Tear gas!" yelled someone.

"The tear gas got into my eyes and lungs," said Joanne Bland, who was ten. "I could not breathe. I could not see."

John Lewis and the others knelt to pray. An officer wearing a gas mask clubbed Lewis on the head. He blacked out. Television cameramen and photographers recorded the violence. Their footage of the day, which became known as "Bloody Sunday," was broadcast that night on major television networks. The brutality outraged many people who did not think this should be happening in America. Large numbers of religious leaders were particularly concerned. Within forty-eight hours ministers, priests, nuns, and rabbis began arriving in Selma to support the movement.

On Tuesday, March 9, Dr. King prepared to lead two thousand demonstrators to the Edmund Pettus Bridge. Lewis was released from the hospital to meet them. But Alabama Governor George Wallace had obtained an order from a

When Anthony Quin, age five, of McComb, Mississippi, refused to give up his small American flag during a voting rights protest, Mississippi Highway Patrolman Huey Krohn wrenched it out of his hands, June 17, 1965.

Participants, including students, carry American flags as they march for civil rights in Selma, Alabama.

federal court in Montgomery prohibiting the march. Dr. King hesitated to break the law. Lewis encouraged him to do it. "The march is legitimate," he said.

President Johnson learned of the tense situation. He instructed his attorney general to ask Dr. King to call off the march because it might lead to another disaster. Dr. King remained worried about breaking the law, but he proceeded anyway. At the end of the bridge he saw a hundred troopers blocking the road. Was it a trap? On the bridge he stopped to pray. Afraid of leading people into another bloodbath, and troubled about disobeying the federal order, he told everyone to turn back. Disappointed protesters dubbed the march "Turn Around Tuesday."

That night James Reeb, a minister from Boston who had come to Selma to join the protests, went out for dinner with two other ministers. Four racist white men attacked them and clubbed Reeb in the head. Reeb was rushed to a hospital and died two days later. The news stunned President Johnson and spurred him into action.

In a televised broadcast on March 15, President Johnson addressed Congress and said, "Every American citizen must have an equal right to vote." He announced that he would be sending a law to Congress "to eliminate illegal barriers" to voting.

"It is the effort of American Negroes to secure for themselves the full blessings of American life," said President Johnson. "Their cause must be our cause too. Because it is not just Negroes, but really it is all of us, who must overcome the crippling legacy of bigotry and injustice." He paused, leaned forward, and slowly said: "And . . . we . . . shall . . . overcome."

Dr. King and John Lewis watched the speech on television. Tears welled up in their eyes. "We will make it from Selma to Montgomery," Dr. King told Lewis, "and the Voting Rights Act will be passed."

Two days later the march was authorized. Governor Wallace refused to provide protection. So President Johnson federalized 1,863 Alabama National Guardsmen to police the route, along with a thousand U.S. Army troops. On Sunday, March 21, thirty-two hundred demonstrators led by Dr. King and Lewis set out in the rain for Montgomery. Jimmie Lee Jackson's eighty-three-year-old grandfather Cager Lee marched with the group. When the procession crossed the county line, the highway narrowed to two lanes, and they were ordered to

Hosea Williams (l.) and John Lewis (r.) leading marchers across the Edmund Pettus Bridge in Selma, Alabama, March 7, 1965.

Alabama state troopers confronting John Lewis and civil rights marchers who have crossed the Edmund Pettus Bridge, in Selma, Alabama, March 7, 1965.

reduce the number of marchers to three hundred. When the road widened to four lanes, hundreds of people rushed to join them, arriving from all over the United States by car, plane, train, and bus.

By the time the marchers reached Montgomery on Thursday, March 25, the throng had swelled to twenty-five thousand. The front line included civil rights

Alabama state troopers attacking civil rights marchers on Bloody Sunday, March 7, 1965.

leaders Rosa Parks, Amelia Boynton, and Coretta Scott King, an activist long before her marriage to Dr. King. They went right up to the state capitol within yards of Governor Wallace's office. He peeked through the venetian blinds and muttered, "That's quite a crowd." Fifteen-year-old Lynda Blackmon, who had marched all the way from Selma, got as close as she could and shouted, "I'm here, Governor Wallace, I'm here!"

After folk singers performed on a makeshift stage, Mrs. Amelia Boynton spoke. Despite blows she had suffered on Bloody Sunday, Mrs. Boynton was able to present a petition demanding an end to discriminatory voting practices in the state. For years she had struggled to teach black people in rural areas of Alabama to fill out forms and become registered voters.

Next, Rosa Parks took the stage and was treated like a star. Mrs. Parks, an icon of the civil rights movement, had refused to give up her seat to a white man on a Montgomery bus in 1955, and had been arrested. Her actions sparked a boycott to fight segregation, led by Dr. King and sustained by Coretta Scott King and groups of black women. Nearly a year later the U.S. Supreme Court ruled that bus segregation was unconstitutional. Now Mrs. Parks, a longtime

John Lewis cringes as an Alabama state trooper swings his club at Lewis's head during the march from Selma to Montgomery, March 7, 1965. Lewis later was admitted to a local hospital with a possible skull fracture.

Amelia Boynton lying on the ground after she and other civil rights marchers were beaten and gassed by state troopers on Bloody Sunday in Selma, Alabama, March 7, 1965.

activist, recalled childhood memories of sitting next to her grandfather, a shotgun across his lap, as the Ku Klux Klan drove by their house.

Finally Dr. King spoke. "They told us we wouldn't get here," he said. "But all the world today knows that we *are* here. . . . We ain't goin' let nobody turn us around."

Dr. Martin Luther King Jr. addressing Selma marchers from the steps of the State Capitol Building in Montgomery, Alabama, March 25, 1965.

CHAPTER 3: NEW VOTERS

"Nobody's free until everybody's free."
—Fannie Lou Hamer (1917–1977), civil rights leader

ON THE MORNING OF AUGUST 6, 1965, PRESIDENT JOHNSON signed the Voting Rights Act (VRA). He invited Dr. King, John Lewis, Rosa Parks, and other civil rights leaders to witness the historic moment. President Johnson used fifty pens to sign the bill, and gave one of them to Lewis, who later framed it and hung it in his living room.

A voter fills out a registration form before a federal registrar in Canton, Mississippi, 1965.

The most important features of the law banned literacy tests and poll taxes. The VRA also authorized the attorney general to appoint federal registrars to monitor elections, particularly in the Deep South, and make sure that citizens were free to register and vote. Any new voting procedures or practices in districts with a history of significant discrimination had to be approved by the U.S. Department of Justice.

On August 10, 1965, Ardies Mauldin, a nurse, and her husband, Thomas, a deliveryman, walked up the steps of the Dallas County Courthouse in Selma to register. A federal examiner's team asked Ardies simple questions, such as her birth date and whether she had ever been convicted of a crime. Within

A voter checks the ballot form before voting in Canton, Mississippi, 1965.

ten minutes they gave her a square white voting certificate with the number 1. Ardies Mauldin was the first voter registered under the VRA. Her husband was the second. "It didn't take but a few minutes," she said. "I don't know why it couldn't have been like that in the first place."

When the Mauldins left the courthouse they passed a line of prospective voters that stretched around the block. That day federal examiners, who had been quickly trained and sent to the South, registered 1,114 black voters in nine counties. Cager Lee, Jimmie Lee Jackson's grandfather, registered to vote for the first time, in Marion, Alabama.

On the second day examiners registered 1,733 voters. In Clinton, Louisiana, Chris Weatherspoon, a sixty-three-year-old farmer, was the first person in line. He had tried to register five times before but the registrar had always said, "Chris, you missed just one word on the [literacy] test." Now, the new federal examiner said to him, "Would you like to register, sir?" Weatherspoon said, "I was praying to the Lord that this time would come."

By August 21 the number of black registered voters had jumped to twenty thousand. "It was clear," reported the *New York Times*, "that something revolutionary was happening in the Deep South."

Fifty-two black candidates qualified to run for office in the 1966 Democratic primaries. Federal observers showed up to monitor the polls. On May 3, Election Day, Cager Lee arrived at the Perry County Courthouse four hours before the polls opened at eight a.m. "I just wanted to make sure I finally [made it here]," he said. And then he voted for the first time.

A tenant farmer in Dallas County walked sixteen miles to cast his ballot. "Man, this is the second emancipation," he said. "I ain't never voted before, but the Lord willing, I sure mean to vote this time."

In Selma, Jim Clark ran for sheriff again against Wilson Baker, the public safety director. Mary Reese, an older black Selma resident, said, "I'm going to vote just as far against Jim Clark as I can anybody in this world. I been waiting him out for a long time. A LONG time."

The sheriff's race was close, but Baker won with enough votes to avoid a runoff. After years of terrorizing people in Selma, Clark lost his job.

In 1967 in Macon County, Alabama, Lucius Amerson, a postman and veteran of the Korean War, became not only the first black sheriff in the South, but the only one in the United States at that time.

"Although I could not register to vote until the age of twenty-one," said Carrie Manuel-Prowell, "I exercise that right because I marched and went to jail for the right to vote. One vote, my vote, counts."

CHAPTER 4: IN THE ROOM WHERE IT HAPPENED

"I agree to this Constitution, with all its faults, if they are such, because I think a general government necessary for us."

—Benjamin Franklin (1706–1790)

WHO DECIDED WHO COULD VOTE IN AMERICA? IN MAY 1787, delegates from twelve states got together to make up the rules. Up till then each state had been writing its own voting laws. In most states only adult free white men who owned property had the privilege of voting. Women and paupers did not. And in some states, neither did Catholics or Jews or free black men.

The delegates, known as the Framers, met in Philadelphia at the State House (now Independence Hall) to write the Constitution of the United States. They were all white men. They sat at thirteen tables, one for each original state, arranged in a semicircle. However, because Rhode Islanders knew that the convention would probably ban their right to issue their own paper money, the Rhode Island table stayed empty. In those days each state set its own value for dollars, and the convention wanted to establish a uniform American currency, which most states agreed was a good idea.

On the opening day the delegates unanimously elected Gen. George Washington as the presiding officer. James Madison took notes as they hammered out the Constitution. Everything that was said "in the room where it happened" was kept secret. Sentries posted at the doors guarded against eavesdropping. Yet passersby could see the delegates through the high windows. So, as the summer

George Washington
by John Roberts, 1799.

dragged on, the windows remained closed despite the heat. Delegates wearing powdered wigs and heavy woolen coats, vests, and waistcoats wiped their brows.

First, they discussed how to elect members of the House of Representatives and the Senate. One option was to base representation on the population of each state. In the South, enslaved people were regarded as property of free individuals rather than as inhabitants. South Carolina proposed the three-fifths clause. According to this provision, five enslaved people would be counted as the equivalent of three free people. Madison and others protested. But the majority of the delegates voted in favor of the three-fifths ratio.

Next came the subject of the presidency. Every delegate and most Americans assumed that Washington would be the first president of the United States. But who would come _after_ Washington? Should a president serve for more than one term? A Maryland delegate suggested a term of eleven years. Another joked, "Twenty years!" The delegates eventually agreed on a term of four years.

But _how_ would U.S. citizens choose a president? Gouverneur Morris of Pennsylvania demanded that the people vote directly. Others complained that a popular election would result in a poor choice. What about letting the people vote for "electors" who would then choose the president? Electors would be wiser than lower-class folks.

What if the president turned out to be a bad one? The Framers agreed that Congress would have the power to impeach a president. He could be put on trial and removed from office if he were convicted of "high crimes and misdemeanors."

After a committee wrote the first draft of the Constitution, the question of who should vote in national elections came up again. Morris declared that only landowners should vote, because poor people would sell their votes to the rich. Others argued that his proposal would "make enemies" of those denied the vote.

The debate then turned to slavery. Many challenged the three-fifths ratio because it would give Southern states too much power. Most of the delegates wanted to ban the slave trade. The issue was so explosive that delegates feared the effort to write the Constitution would fall apart. They then made what proved to be one of the most controversial and morally problematic decisions in U.S. history: they refrained from addressing the issue. The word *slavery* did not even appear in the Constitution.

In late August the convention discussed the presidency again. A motion that the president be chosen "by the people" was turned down. Morris again raised the idea that the people could vote for electors who would then choose the president. Everyone agreed. Electors would meet in their states and cast their ballots. The ballots would be sent to Congress and tallied up. The person with the most electoral votes would be president, and the runner-up would be vice president.

Next, a Committee of Style that included Morris, Madison, and Alexander Hamilton edited the Constitution and polished the wording. They wanted the document to be short and allow room for growth. Morris rewrote the preamble. He changed "We the People of the States of New Hampshire, Massachusetts, Rhode Island" and so on, to "We the People of *the*

Alexander Hamilton by John Trumbull, 1804–06.

Depiction of the Committee on Style for the U.S. Constitution, 1787.

Benjamin Franklin by Joseph Siffred Duplessis, c. 1785.

United States." This acknowledged Americans as individual citizens with rights.

On September 17, Madison read the final Constitution aloud. Afterward, Benjamin Franklin gave a speech saying that he did not approve of several parts and found "errors." Nevertheless, he said, "I agree to this Constitution, with all its faults, if they are such, because I think a general government necessary for us."

Washington signed the document first. Then thirty-eight other delegates from twelve states added their names. Copies of the Constitution were immediately sent to the states for approval. Three-fourths needed to approve the document before it could go into effect. On June 21, 1788, New Hampshire, the ninth state necessary for ratification, gave its endorsement .

Although the preamble began "We the people of the United States," the

Scene at the Signing of the Constitution of the United States by Howard Chandler Christy, 1940. The painting depicts Independence Hall in Philadelphia on September 17, 1787. George Washington stands on the platform. Benjamin Franklin is seated in the center with Alexander Hamilton leaning toward him.

states had the power to decide who "the people" were. The Constitution did not grant any individuals the right to vote. Presidents would be chosen by electors. And each state would decide how to appoint those electors. So, despite a new set of rules for America, political power remained in the hands of relatively few people. Voters were still wealthy white men, many of whom were slaveholders. Should these people be the only ones to vote?

CHAPTER 5: WHO IS ENTITLED TO VOTE?

"A voteless people were a hopeless people."
—Mrs. Amelia Boynton (1911–2015), civil rights leader

THE CONSTITUTION HAD DEFECTS, AND THE BILL OF RIGHTS and other amendments came quickly. The Twelfth Amendment, in 1803, concerned voting. Before this amendment, the person who won the most votes became president, and the runner-up became vice president. Now electors in each state cast one vote for president and a separate vote for vice president.

But who was entitled to choose the electors? Free white men, of course, who owned property, paid taxes, and had lived in the state for at least a year. Many Americans thought this wasn't fair. Just because a person owned a large piece of land didn't make him "wiser or better."

Soldiers who had risked their lives fighting in the Revolutionary War and the War of 1812 believed that they should have the right to vote. Tenant farmers, who rented their land, thought they should too. So did mechanics and shopkeepers. Immigrants settling in cities and towns also wanted to vote. A Boston newspaper, the *Daily Advertiser and Courier*, declared, "The mass of the people are honest and capable of self-government."

Many states dropped the property qualifications for voting for governor and other state officials. Residency requirements were shortened so that immigrants could cast their ballots. Enslaved people in the South were still counted as property and could not vote. Every state that entered the Union after 1819 banned black people from voting. Northern states such as New Jersey, Maryland, and Connecticut that had permitted black men to vote during the first years of independence now limited suffrage (the right to vote) to whites. In 1838, the supreme court of Pennsylvania ruled that black men could not vote because

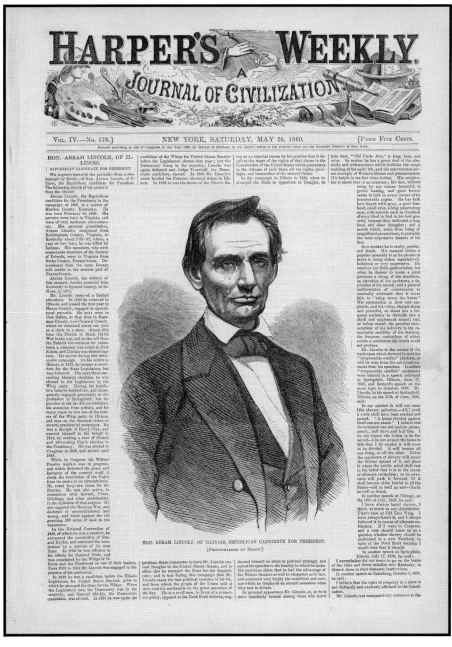

HARPER'S WEEKLY.

A JOURNAL OF CIVILIZATION

VOL. IV.—No. 178.]   NEW YORK, SATURDAY, MAY 26, 1860.   [PRICE FIVE CENTS.

Entered according to Act of Congress, in the Year 1860, by Harper & Brothers, in the Clerk's Office of the District Court for the Southern District of New York.

HON. ABRAM LINCOLN, OF ILLINOIS, REPUBLICAN CANDIDATE FOR PRESIDENT.

[PHOTOGRAPHED BY BRADY.]

Abraham Lincoln pictured in *Harper's Weekly*, May 26, 1860, after he had secured the Republican Party's nomination for president.

they were not "freemen." By 1855 all but five states discriminated against African Americans.

In 1862, during the Civil War, President Abraham Lincoln issued a preliminary Emancipation Proclamation setting a date for freeing enslaved people. It would go into effect if the Confederate states stopped rebelling. They did

Tintype portrait of United States Colored Troops soldier William Johnson from Kentucky, ca. 1865.

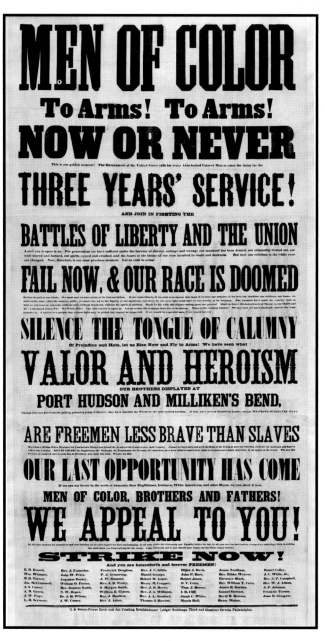

A broadside poster written by Frederick Douglass encouraging "Men of Color" to enlist in the army, 1863.

not. So in 1863 Lincoln issued the final Emancipation Proclamation. However, it did not free all slaves—five hundred thousand enslaved people in the border states of Missouri, Kentucky, Maryland, and Delaware remained in bondage. The proclamation also called for establishing black military units, and thousands of black men joined the Union Army and Navy. In 1864 President Lincoln proposed the Thirteenth Amendment, which would abolish slavery. After the war ended, Congress passed the amendment, and it was ratified by the states on December 6, 1865.

Men who had been enslaved expected to have the right to vote. Many of them had revolted during the war and had served with the Union Army. In January 1866, the National Convention of Colored Men gathered in Washington, D.C., to ask President Andrew Johnson to help them. Johnson, who had succeeded Lincoln, refused. He told a delegation headed by Frederick Douglass, a formerly enslaved man, that granting suffrage to black people was a "hollow, unpractical idea" that would "cause great injury to the white and colored man." President Johnson despised Douglass, whose brilliant writing had made him a celebrity. The president said that if the delegation pursued its goals of equality, it would cause a "race war." He suggested that the only good solution was for black people to leave the country.

Douglass shot back that a race war in the Southern states could only be avoided by granting black suffrage. After the meeting Douglass wrote a powerful speech and took it on the road from Brooklyn to St. Louis. He declared, "Slavery is not abolished until the black man has the ballot."

In 1868, Congress finally passed the Fourteenth Amendment. The amendment gave the vote to male U.S. citizens at least twenty-one years old. It also declared that formerly enslaved people born in the United States were citizens. However, it did not adequately protect their right to vote.

At last, in 1869, the Fifteenth Amendment was passed, and it was ratified in 1870. It prohibited the federal or state government from denying any American the right to vote because "of race, color, or previous condition of servitude." Not only could black men vote, they could also run for office. Hiram Rhodes Revels, a pastor and educator who had been born a free man, became the first black senator in the United States. Revels won a seat in the Senate representing Mississippi.

Matthew Washington Gaines, a minister who had been enslaved and had escaped his master twice, was elected to the Texas Senate. Senator Gaines crusaded for education

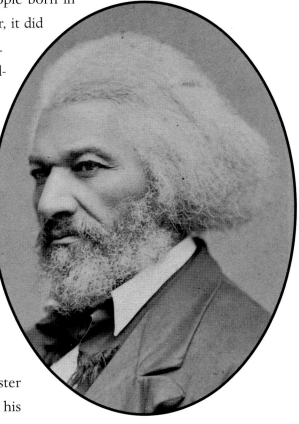

Photograph of Frederick Douglass by George Kendall Warren, 1876.

A lithograph depicting a parade in celebration of the passing of the Fifteenth Amendment.

for black people and encouraged them to take part in public life. And large numbers of black people did. Over the next few years as many as two thousand black people throughout the South served as state legislators, justices of the peace, and sheriffs.

But this period of political activity for black citizens soon ended. White supremacists, who believed whites were inherently superior to all other races and should be in complete authority, formed terrorist groups such as the Ku Klux Klan to intimidate black voters. White legislators dreamed up literacy tests and poll taxes to prevent black people from registering to vote. New laws gave local registrars total control over who could and could not vote. A Mississippi official said, "The plan is to invest permanently the powers of government in the hands of the people who ought to have them—the white people."

White authorities tried their best to restrict access to education for black people. They particularly wanted to suppress widespread knowledge of the fact that black people had equal rights according to the Fifteenth Amendment to the Constitution.

In the twentieth century, the civil rights movement took hold and fought to change the system. Civil rights activists helped inform black people of their rights. Amelia Boynton and her husband, leaders in the Voters League, came to Selma, Alabama, in 1929 and were appalled. "It was devastating to see black people still enslaved!" said Mrs. Boynton. "My husband truly believed that a voteless people were a hopeless people."

CHAPTER 6: WHEN WE ALL VOTE

"I labor under the double handicap of race and sex."
—Mary Church Terrell (1863–1954), women's suffragist

IN THE EIGHTEENTH CENTURY, WOMEN WERE CONSIDERED family members who depended on their husbands and fathers to protect them and defend their interests. If unmarried women had property, it automatically was transferred to their husbands when they wed. According to the Constitution, free men over the age of twenty-one who owned property were the only people qualified to vote. But many women, such as Abigail Adams, wanted to have a voice in the laws that governed them.

"Remember the Ladies," wrote Adams to her husband, John, who was a representative to the Continental Congress in 1776. "Do not put such unlimited power into the hands of the Husbands [as your ancestors did]. . . . If perticuliar care and attention is not paid to the Laidies we are determined to foment a Rebelion, and will not hold ourselves bound by any Laws in which we have no voice, or Representation."

Of course Abigail Adams was referring to the wives of white male Patriots, but black women felt the same way. They carried the added burden of confronting racism while seeking empowerment. John Adams jokingly wrote to his wife that her letter made him laugh. He noted that the Patriots' struggle had evidently stirred up discontent and had now "stimulated" white women to "demand new Priviledges." He ignored her advice, as did the other Founding Fathers. Eventually women rebelled.

An organized movement to give *white* women the vote began in July 1848 at a convention in Seneca Falls, New York. There were more than three hundred attendees, both women and men. No black women attended the convention. None were invited.

Elizabeth Cady Stanton and Lucretia Mott led the way. These suffragists drew up a Declaration of Sentiments that called for equality for women. The most important point demanded that women have the right to vote. Stanton's husband was so shocked by the idea that he left town during the meeting. But Frederick Douglass, an African American friend of Mrs. Stanton's, was there, and he spoke in support of women's right to vote. Sixty-eight women and thirty-two men at the convention signed the declaration. They petitioned state legislatures to reform laws, and argued that women were the equals of men. Stanton and Mott began to see the similarity between their plight and that of enslaved people who had no control over their lives.

At a women's rights convention in 1851 in Akron, Ohio, Sojourner

Abolitionist and women's rights activist Sojourner Truth with a photograph of her grandson, James Caldwell of Co. H, 54th Massachusetts Infantry Regiment, on her lap. Caldwell was a prisoner of war at James Island, South Carolina, between 1863 and 1865.

Truth, a black abolitionist, gave a powerful speech. Truth had been born into slavery in New York, where slavery was not completely abolished until 1827, and had escaped with her infant daughter. However, as time went on, Truth distanced herself from most women's rights groups because of racist remarks made by leaders such as Susan B. Anthony. Historians have revealed that Stanton was bigoted too, privately characterizing African American men as "Sambos."

After the Civil War broke out in 1861, Northern women put aside their struggle in order to support the war effort. When the war ended, the women resumed their campaign to win the vote. But the government ignored their pleas as it passed new laws. The Fourteenth Amendment promised male citizens over the age of twenty-one the right to vote. The Fifteenth Amendment gave "citizens of the United States" the right to vote regardless of "race, color, or previous condition of servitude." Women believed they were citizens too. They pointed out that Webster's dictionary defined an American citizen as someone entitled to vote and hold real estate. Many men agreed.

Eli T. Blackmer, superintendent of public schools in San Diego, said, "Whatever rights are given to one citizen ought to be given . . . to every other citizen." Some men maintained that women had special qualities and virtues that would bring "integrity and honesty" to politics. Many believed that the presence of women would end "scoundrelism and ruffianism at the polls."

Stanton and Anthony formed the National Woman Suffrage Association (NWSA) to protest the Fifteenth Amendment. White women deserved the vote ahead of formerly enslaved black men, they said. Many of Anthony's statements make her prejudice against black people clear. Once she said she would rather "cut off this right arm of mine before I will ever work or demand the ballot for the Negro and not the woman."

Stanton, the mother of seven children, wrote speeches for Anthony to deliver. Sometimes Anthony, who was single, helped Stanton with household chores so that she could write. "You must make the puddings and carry the baby while I ply the pen," said Stanton to Anthony.

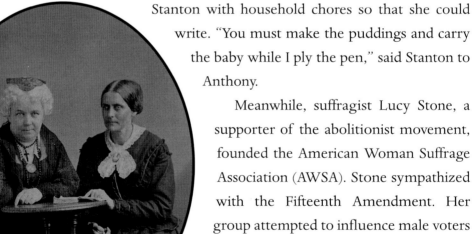

Meanwhile, suffragist Lucy Stone, a supporter of the abolitionist movement, founded the American Woman Suffrage Association (AWSA). Stone sympathized with the Fifteenth Amendment. Her group attempted to influence male voters to expand the rights of women, at least in state elections. She offered advice for wives: "When he says good morning, tell him you want to vote; when he asks what you are going to have for dinner, tell him you want to vote; and whatever he asks from the time

Elizabeth Cady Stanton (l.) and Susan B. Anthony, women's suffrage leaders.

you rise up in the morning until you lie down at night, tell him you want to vote."

Hardly any of these measures that were aimed at giving women voting rights made it onto a state ballot. A few states and territories gave women "partial suffrage" in local elections concerning education and liquor licenses. In Kentucky, widows with property and even unmarried women could vote in school elections.

In 1869 two elderly sisters, Abbey and Julia Smith, held their own personal rebellion. They refused to pay taxes on their farm in Glastonbury, Connecticut, until the town allowed them to vote. The sisters' rebellion went on for years. Finally the tax assessor came to their farm and seized their cows in payment for back taxes. Although the sisters won their case in court and got their property back, they still could not vote.

In 1869, however, Wyoming passed a law giving women full civil equality with men. On the morning of September 6, 1870, Louisa Ann Gardner Swain walked to downtown Laramie to buy some yeast and passed the polling place. It had not yet opened, but election officials invited her to come in and cast her ballot. She did, and was the first woman in the United States to vote in a general election.

In Colorado, activist Elizabeth Piper Ensley organized African American women to win suffrage. Ensley, a teacher and librarian from the East, had taught at Howard University in Washington, D.C., with her husband before moving to Denver in 1892. At that time Denver was segregated, and Ensley worked hard to bring about social change. As treasurer of the Colorado Non-Partisan Equal Suffrage Association, she campaigned to put the women's suffrage amendment on the 1893 ballot and succeeded. On September 7, 1893, women won the right to vote in Colorado, and they cast their ballots in the 1894 election.

Many men feared giving women the vote. A Pennsylvania politician said that if women could vote, "the family . . . would be utterly destroyed." There would be arguments between husbands and wives. "The whole country—every household would or might be the scene of everlasting quarrels," he predicted.

Some men thought that women shouldn't participate in the "rough and tumble" world of politics. Only the "worst" women would vote and thus degrade themselves. Still others maintained that the right to vote ought to be linked to

Carrie Chapman Catt, campaigner for the Nineteenth Amendment.

military service. There were even women who opposed suffrage, saying they preferred using their influence behind the scenes.

By 1890 no real progress had been made. So the two competing organizations, the AWSA and the NWSA, merged into the National American Woman Suffrage Association (NAWSA). Carrie Chapman Catt, a teacher and school administrator from Iowa, took over as leader. Catt excelled at organizing and strategizing. She established headquarters in every state, and coordinated campaigns. She published pamphlets. She targeted upper-class white women for donations. Catt said, "Women are not in rebellion against men. They are in rebellion against wornout traditions."

But African American women were not allowed to take part in the NAWSA. So Ida B. Wells, a civil rights activist and journalist, teamed up with her white colleagues Belle Squire and Virginia Brooks and established the Alpha Suffrage Club in Chicago. Members knew they not only had to fight for the right to vote, but the ability to exercise that right without intimidation.

Wells was from the South, where terrorist groups like the Ku Klux Klan stabbed, whipped, and murdered black

Ida B. Wells—journalist, educator, and activist for civil and women's rights—was one of the founders of the National Association for the Advancement of Colored People.

Young African American suffragists appear in an August 1915 *Crisis* magazine article "Votes for Women."

men who dared try to vote. After three of her friends in Memphis, Tennessee, had been lynched for competing with white businessmen, Wells began to investigate lynching. Her published exposé *Southern Horrors* enraged locals, and death threats forced her to move to Chicago. There she married African American lawyer Ferdinand Barnett and continued to fight for civil rights and women's suffrage.

Another new suffragist was Alice Paul. Paul traveled to London, England, to study social work, and became a suffragette (the British term for women fighting for voting rights). She was arrested seven times and met Lucy Burns, a fellow American suffragette, at a police station. Burns and Paul became friends and joined forces back in the United States.

At first Paul became active in NAWSA, but feeling it was too tame, she broke off from it and formed what became the National Woman's Party. Paul and Burns organized a suffrage parade in Washington, D.C., on March 3, 1913, the day before President Woodrow Wilson's inauguration.

When white Southern women heard that black women were going to join the procession, they refused to participate. Paul did not want the race issue to spoil the event, so she suggested that African American women march as a group at the back of the parade instead of with their state delegations. Nearly everyone was offended.

Mary Church Terrell, an advocate of women's suffrage and civil rights.

Weeks before the parade, an African American sorority at Howard University, Delta Sigma Theta, asked to march with the college women. They were represented by an honorary member, Mary Church Terrell. Terrell, a black activist, had moved to Washington when she married Robert Heberton Terrell, a lawyer. Since her days at Oberlin College in Ohio, Terrell had believed in suffrage and had written the Delta Sigma Theta creed: "I labor under the double handicap of race and sex."

Terrell accepted Paul's compromise of allowing their group to march with the New York City Woman Suffrage Party. The sorority was the only African American women's organization that took part.

On the day of the march, Ida B. Wells arrived in Washington with sixty-two

Inez Milholland Boissevain, a young attorney, riding a white horse at the head of the March 3, 1913, Women's Suffrage Parade in Washington, D.C.

Suffragists, dressed in white, marching in the Women's Suffrage Parade in Washington, D.C., March 3, 1913.

other Illinois suffragists, all white. Paul didn't want Wells to march with her delegation. She wanted to keep it all white. The Illinois delegates objected and said they wanted to have Wells with them. Paul said no. In a trembling voice Wells said, "If the Illinois women do not take a stand now in this great democratic

American nurses marching in the Women's Suffrage Parade in Washington, D.C., March 3, 1913.

parade, then the colored women are lost." She said she would not march at all unless she could be with her state delegates. Two of the Illinois women offered to march with her in the African American section, but Wells had walked away.

The march started. The women formed their ranks. And when the Illinois group lined up, Wells suddenly appeared and assumed her place with them. A photographer from Chicago's *Daily Tribune* snapped a picture of her.

Eight thousand women and girls showed up to participate. Inez Milholland Boissevain, an attorney, dressed in white and riding a white horse, headed the parade from the Capitol to the White House. Women followed behind her holding a banner that read WE DEMAND AN AMENDMENT TO THE CONSTITUTION OF THE UNITED STATES ENFRANCHISING THE WOMEN OF THE COUNTRY. Wives and daughters of congressmen marched, along with teachers, doctors, nurses, artists, and business leaders. The women wore sashes and carried flags featuring the organization's colors: purple, gold, and white.

Violence erupted minutes after the parade began. Spectators, mostly men, shouted insults. Some tried to climb aboard the floats. Policemen did little to protect the marchers. One officer said, "There would be nothing like this if you women would all stay at home."

Finally, National Guard troops arrived to control the riot. The next day the youngest daughter of Elizabeth Cady Stanton, one of the original suffragists, sent a telegram to President Wilson. It read: "Yesterday the government, which is supposed to exist for the good of all, left women . . . at the mercy of a howling mob." The president did not respond.

But newspaper coverage exceeded Alice Paul's greatest expectations. Public sympathy was aroused. She realized the power of the press to advance their cause, and wrote, "This mistreatment by the police was probably the best thing that could ever have happened to us."

CHAPTER 7: SILENT SENTINELS

"I should be proud to die in prison for the liberty of American women."

—Mary A. Nolan (1842–1925), women's suffragist

AFTER THE PARADE, ALICE PAUL AND LUCY BURNS continued their campaign for an amendment to the Constitution. In 1914, U.S. senators held their first vote on the measure. A third of the senators abstained. Despite a one-vote majority, there were not enough senators to give the necessary two-thirds majority. Later when the House of Representatives held a vote on women's suffrage, the measure also failed.

With so many defeats, Paul and her staff asked Carrie Catt to take charge. Catt organized state chapters of the NAWSA to lobby for women's suffrage. At a meeting of NAWSA leaders, President Wilson said to them, "I have not come to ask you to be patient, because you have been." Yet he added, "You can afford a little while to wait." Former NAWSA president Anna Howard Shaw responded, "We have waited so long, Mr. President, for the vote—and we had hoped it might come in your administration."

Suffragist Alice Paul leading a picket line from National Woman's Party headquarters, October 1917.

The first suffrage campaign pickets leaving Cameron House, headquarters of the Congressional Union, before heading to the White House, January 1917.

But the president refused to endorse suffrage.

So in January 1917, Paul organized a picket line in front of the White House. This was the first time in American history that citizens staged a nonviolent political protest there. Twelve suffragists carried banners printed with their urgent questions:

HOW LONG MUST WOMEN WAIT FOR LIBERTY?

MR. PRESIDENT, WHAT WILL YOU DO FOR WOMAN SUFFRAGE?

Over the next year, women ranging in age from nineteen to eighty took turns picketing. Thousands participated. Among them was African American suffragist Mary Church Terrell. When she had moved to Washington she had been appalled to find segregation in the nation's capital, and had worked to "promote the welfare" of her race. Terrell served as the first president of the National Association of Colored Women, and then joined the National Association for the Advancement of Colored People (NAACP). As a good friend of Carrie Catt's, Terrell fought for female suffrage in general, and the rights of black women in particular.

That winter of 1916–1917, Terrell received phone calls from the headquarters of the National Woman's Party asking her to come and picket at the White House. She went, leaving her warm, comfortable home, and often took her nineteen-year-old daughter, Phyllis, with her to "swell the numbers." Terrell remembered how she and Phyllis stood on hot bricks supplied by a black man to "keep our their feet from freezing."

Also prominent among the group of picketers was Rose Winslow, a Polish immigrant and labor organizer, actress, and poet who brought her considerable skills to the suffrage movement. Some joined the line on a whim while they visited Washington, and a few even picketed during their honeymoons. Supporters brought hot coffee, flowers, and more heated bricks for the women to stand on in cold weather. Since nothing like this had ever happened before, President Wilson didn't know what to do. At first he tipped his hat to the ladies when he passed by. He instructed White House guards to offer coffee to the "Silent Sentinels," as they were known, but the women declined. By the time of his second inauguration, on March 4, 1917, President Wilson had lost patience with the picketers. The suffragists had lost patience too, and organized a "grand picket." On Inauguration Day they marched around the White House for two hours in drenching rain.

At that point a dozen countries in Europe were engaged in the Great War, later called World War I. In April, the president asked Congress to declare war

Suffragists picketing at the White House stood on hot bricks to stay warm.

Representatives of colleges and universities picket in front of the White House on College Day, February 1917, and remind President Wilson that women want the vote.

on Germany. "The world must be made safe for democracy," he said, and the United States entered the conflict.

Once again, some of the suffragists put aside their own campaign to do war work too—but not all, including Alice Paul. "We have no true democracy in this country, though we are fighting for democracy abroad," she said. "Twenty million American citizens are denied a voice in their own government." She and others picketed the White House as well as the Capitol. Public opinion turned against her and deemed her actions "unwomanly" and "unpatriotic."

Starting in June 1917, twenty-seven of her picketers were arrested on grounds of "causing a crowd to gather and thus obstructing traffic." Six were tried and convicted. They had a choice of paying a $25 fine (about $520 today) or spending three days in jail. The women would not pay, so they became the first suffragists in the United States to be jailed.

In July ten more women were arrested and jailed. On July 14, Bastille Day— French independence day—the picketers carried a banner with the French motto: Liberty, Equality, Fraternity. A mob formed around them. Boys hurled insults, and snatched the banners and destroyed them. Police arrested sixteen women picketers, including grandmothers. When the judge gave them a choice of a $25 fine or sixty days at the Occoquan Workhouse in Virginia, the women chose the workhouse. By chance, Mary Church Terrell had not been able to picket that day and was spared the horrors of Occoquan.

Conditions there were gruesome. The "jailbirds," as they called themselves, were issued shoes—one-size-fits-all—and filthy blankets, and fed bread and water and sometimes worm-infested soup. A bucket served as a toilet, and rats scampered in the shadows. But the women sang to each other to keep up their spirits, and those who knew foreign languages taught classes.

Over the summer and into the fall of 1917, suffragists picketed, and more than two hundred were arrested. By October, when Congress prepared to adjourn, lawmakers had not acted on the suffrage amendment. Alice Paul joined the picket line, was arrested, and was sent to the District of Columbia Jail.

"Dear Mother," she wrote, "I have been sentenced today to seven months imprisonment. Please do not worry. It will merely be a delightful rest."

She was dead wrong. Paul was put into an airless cell with eighty other prisoners. "I went to a window and tried to open it," she recalled. "Instantly a group of men, prison guards, appeared; picked me up bodily, threw me into a cell and locked the door." The guards had placed her in solitary confinement.

Her fellow suffragists in neighboring cells, including Rose Winslow, organized a rebellion with her, demanding the rights of political prisoners. As such they would be entitled to eat nourishing food, send and receive mail, exercise outdoors, and meet with their lawyers. They had offended the administration politically, but were not criminals who had broken the law. "We determined to make it impossible to keep us in jail," Paul recalled. When Paul entered the jail she weighed less than a hundred pounds, and couldn't chew the salt pork that was part of the prison diet.

Paul grew weaker. After two weeks she and Winslow, who had also been in solitary, were carried on stretchers to the prison hospital. They began a hunger strike. As a punishment, prison officials put Paul in a psychiatric ward and tried to prove that she was insane. They woke her up every hour and deprived her of sleep. When she still refused to eat, they force-fed her by sticking a tube down her throat into her stomach.

Winslow suffered the same ordeal, and scribbled notes to her husband on scraps of paper that were smuggled out. "Yesterday was a bad day for me in feeding," she wrote. "I was vomiting continually during the process. . . . The same doctor feeds both Alice Paul and me. Don't let them tell you we take this well. . . . We think of the coming feeding all day. It is horrible.

"All the officers here know we are making this hunger strike so that women fighting for liberty may be considered political prisoners," wrote Winslow. "God knows we don't want other women ever to have to do this again."

But many other women did.

CHAPTER 8: JAILBIRDS

"Night of terror."

—Doris Stevens (1888–1963), women's suffragist, author
of *Jailed for Freedom*

SUFFRAGISTS HEARD ABOUT THE TREATMENT ALICE PAUL and Rose Winslow had suffered. In protest, forty-one women formed a picket line, the longest yet, in front of the White House. They were all arrested and sent to the Occoquan Workhouse. The youngest was nineteen, and the oldest was Mrs. Mary Nolan, age seventy-three.

The women arrived at night. Prison guards shoved them into cells and knocked them down. "A man came at me and caught me by the shoulder," recalled Mrs. Nolan. "I'll come with you; don't drag me," she said. "I have a lame foot." But he jerked her down the steps and rushed her into a "filthy" stone "punishment" cell. It had an "iron bed covered with a thin straw pad, and an open toilet flushed from outside the cell." The men who ran the prison wanted to "break the wills of these well-to-do white ladies."

The details of the treatment of the women at the Occoquan Workhouse are known today because of Doris Stevens. A teacher, social worker, and organizer for the NAWSA, Stevens was arrested with the other picketers. In 1920 she published a meticulous account of her imprisonment called *Jailed for Freedom*.

Lucy Burns tried to do a roll call of the prisoners. Guards handcuffed her with her arms raised, and chained her to the cell door for the rest of the night. The jailers threw Mrs. Dora Lewis, a renowned NAWSA organizer, into the cell. Her head hit the iron bed. "We thought she was dead," said Mrs. Nolan. "She didn't move. We were crying over her as we lifted her to the pad on my bed." The superintendent stormed angrily at them. He ordered them to shut up or he'd gag them and put them into straitjackets.

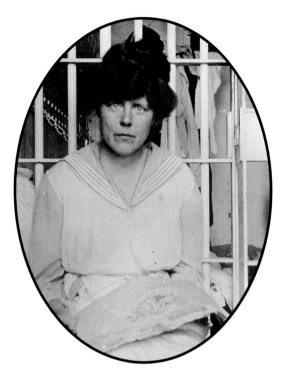

Lucy Burns, suffragist, sits in front of a prison cell, wearing a standard white prison uniform. Burns spent more time in jail than any other member of the National Woman's Party.

During the "night of terror" another suffragist had a heart attack. Mrs. Nolan and the others called to the guards to get a doctor, but they paid no attention.

The next day the suffragists' lawyer attempted to see them but was denied admission. Lucy Burns smuggled out reports about their brutal treatment. Their lawyer forced his way into the prison with a court order and was horrified to hear about the "unknown tortures going on." He brought the news to NAWSA headquarters.

Meanwhile, the women fought back by going on a hunger strike. Burns and Mrs. Lewis were taken to an operating room and held down for force-feedings. Elizabeth McShane, a former school principal, described the process: a doctor poured a pint of cold milk mixed with raw eggs into a tube inserted down the prisoner's throat.

Burns wouldn't open her mouth, so the doctor pushed the tube up her nose. "Operation leaves one very sick," she recalled. "Food dumped directly into stomach feels like a ball of lead." On the seventh day, Mrs. Lewis and Burns, considered the leaders, were taken to the D.C. Jail in Washington. That was where the judge had originally sentenced the women to serve their terms.

In the meantime, the condition of the suffragists at the workhouse grew worse. Finally, their lawyer brought their case to the attention of President Wilson. The president sent a prison commissioner to the workhouse to investigate. The commissioner lied and reported that nothing was wrong. He said the prisoners even cooperated with the force-feedings.

At last the suffrage lawyers arranged a hearing for the workhouse prisoners before a Virginia judge. On November 23, 1917, the trial took place. The purpose was to determine the legality of sending the women to the workhouse.

TORTURING WOMEN IN PRISON

Votes for Women

PUBLISHED BY THE NATIONAL WOMEN'S SOCIAL AND POLITICAL UNION 4 CLEMENTS INN STRAND W.C. & PRINTED BY DAVID ALLEN & SONS L.D. 186 FLEET ST E.C.

VOTE AGAINST THE GOVERNMENT

A poster protesting forced feeding as a punishment shows the interior of a prison cell where a woman is being held seated in a chair while a man pours liquid into a tube inserted in her nose.

Newspaper reporters and spectators packed the room. Everyone was stunned when the women staggered in. Some were so weak that they stretched out on the wooden benches and couldn't sit up. "Still others bore the marks of the attack on the 'night of terror,'" wrote Doris Stevens. The lawyers argued that the women should never have been sent to the workhouse in Virginia. They had been charged with committing crimes in Washington, and should have been imprisoned there. The judge agreed. Within five days President Wilson pardoned all the women.

Now the suffragists claimed they had been jailed unjustly. They had not broken any laws. Why were they charged with "obstructing sidewalk traffic"

Dora Lewis, one of the suffragists arrested in August 1918 and sent to a dilapidated jail in Washington, D.C., is shown being supported on the day of her release, the fifth day of her hunger strike.

In December 1918 Alice Paul and one hundred other suffragists jailed for picketing the White House were each given a Jail Door pin, designed by Nina Allender. This original pin, owned by suffragist Betsy Graves Reyneau, who was arrested on July 14, 1917, and imprisoned for four days, was passed from one feminist to another.

when it was the mob who had caused the riot? Why hadn't the police controlled the crowds? The suffragists demanded that their records be cleared, and they sued the workhouse superintendent, the warden, and a guard.

The suffragists hoped their ordeal and the surrounding publicity would lead to change. However, when Congress reconvened in December, President Wilson delivered a speech without mentioning the suffrage amendment. He had more urgent problems. The president had to build up the army and navy to send an independent American Expeditionary Force to Europe. The Allies needed the help of American troops to battle the Germans.

By this point, the suffragists had drawn national attention to their cause. The jailbirds traveled throughout the country giving speeches. They entertained crowds with prison songs, and dropped leaflets from their chartered trains. By increasing public awareness they hoped to gain support for suffrage and influence legislators to pass the amendment.

In early December 1918, the National Woman's Party honored the jailbirds at a mass meeting and presented each one with a silver pin. The pin resembled a tiny cell door bound by a chain and a heart-shaped lock. "It was a badge of courage given to those who had been jailed for freedom," recalled a party member.

The audience cheered and immediately pledged thousands of dollars to continue the campaign. How long would it take for the government to pass the amendment giving women the right to vote?

CHAPTER 9: THE BURNING INDIGNATION OF WOMEN

"Hurrah and vote for Suffrage."

—Phoebe Ensminger Burn (1873–1945), educator

ON JANUARY 9, 1918, PRESIDENT WILSON FINALLY DECLARED his support of women's suffrage. The work women were doing for the war effort—selling bonds, distributing food, knitting clothes, and giving gifts to the soldiers and sailors—had softened his heart, and he expressed his gratitude. "We have made partners of the women in this war," he told a committee of Democratic congressmen. "This war could not have been fought . . . if it had not been for the services of women." The next day, the House of Representatives began considering the amendment to give women the right to vote. At last the measure passed!

But the Nineteenth Amendment still had to pass in the Senate during the same legislative session. In Washington, Carrie Catt and Alice Paul lobbied senators for their support. Mary Church Terrell delivered political speeches and worked with black women's groups. Former president Theodore Roosevelt jumped in to help, and tried to convince Republican senators to approve the amendment.

Meanwhile, the country was concerned with the war overseas. Newspapers printed daily accounts of battles, illustrated with maps and photos. In June, Gen. John J. Pershing had arrived in England with his independent American Expeditionary Force. By October, American troops were fighting in the trenches on the Western Front alongside their British, French, Belgian, and Portuguese allies.

Sacrifices at home helped the country support the troops. The *Chicago Tribune* printed a recipe for Loyalty Bread: "Save a Loaf a Week: Help Win the

War." The recipe called for substituting wheat flour with tapioca, buckwheat flour, and corn meal so that more bread could be sent to the troops in Europe. Thousands of American soldiers were wounded and died. Women lost their sons, brothers, husbands, fathers, and nephews. But the fresh American troops boosted the Allies' morale, and they started to defeat the Central Powers of Germany, Austria-Hungary, Bulgaria, and the Ottoman Empire.

Back in the United States, tallies showed that the Nineteenth Amendment was two votes short of passage in the Senate. To pressure the Senate, Alice Paul staged a demonstration at a statue honoring the Marquis de Lafayette, the French general who had helped America during the Revolutionary War. As soon as Paul started speaking, police officers arrested her and forty-eight other suffragists. The charge? "Holding a meeting in public grounds" and "climbing on a statue." The convicted women refused to pay a fine, so they were sent to the D.C. Jail.

"The place was the worst the women had experienced," recalled Doris Stevens. The jail had damp cells that smelled of sewer gas. Contaminated drinking water from old rusty pipes made the women "violently ill," and rats ran everywhere. "As a kind of relief from the revolting odors, the prisoners took their straw pallets from the cells to the floor outside," wrote Stevens. "They were ordered back to their cells but refused in a body to go. They preferred the stone floors to the vile odors within." All but two of them went on a hunger strike. When senators came to visit their constituents, they were shocked by the atrocious conditions, and complained to the authorities. By the fifth day the prisoners were released.

But senators threatened to recess without voting on the amendment. So the suffragists returned to Lafayette Square and torched a copy of the president's pledge to urge passage of the amendment. A suffragist cried, "The torch which I hold symbolizes the burning indignation of the women who for years have been given words without action."

Senators voted on the amendment on October 1. However, it failed to pass by two votes. Election Day was weeks away. Suffragists picketed the White House to persuade the Senate to review its vote. Despite their efforts, the Senate recessed in November without reconsidering women's suffrage.

On November 11, 1918, World War I ended. GREAT WAR OVER, proclaimed

The "night of terror" in Occoquan Workhouse, November 1917.
The women inmates rest on straw mats outside their cells.

the *San Francisco Chronicle* on its front page. WAR HAS BEEN WON AND PEACE IS HERE, announced the *New York Daily News*. President Wilson sailed to France to take part in peace talks. At a torchlit ceremony in Washington D.C., Olympia Brown, an eighty-four-year-old suffragist, declared, "I have fought for liberty for seventy years. I protest against the president leaving our country with this old fight here unwon."

Nonetheless, by the end of 1918 fifteen of the forty-eight states—the number at that time—had granted women full suffrage rights. But what about women in the other states? Paul expressed her frustration by burning the president's speeches on democracy in front of the White House. She and dozens of other suffragists were arrested and jailed. When the president heard about it he began pressuring anti-suffrage Democratic senators to change their votes.

A new Senate vote was set for February 2, 1919. The measure lost by one vote. When President Wilson returned from France, Paul welcomed him at the dock in Boston with yet another protest. She and twenty other suffragists were arrested and spent eight days in the Charles Street Jail. As further punishment, some of the suffragists lost their jobs. One woman was disowned by her father, and another was divorced by her husband on the grounds that she had disgraced him.

Congress adjourned on March 3, 1919, without looking at the amendment again. Now both houses of Congress would have to pass the measure again before it could be ratified by the states. Only one vote was needed. President

Wilson sailed back to Europe. But while he was away he recruited a new senator from Georgia to cast the winning vote. Using his executive powers, the president called Congress into a special session. By May 21, the House of Representatives had approved the amendment. On June 4, 1919, the Senate held its final vote and approved it with two extra votes. But the fight wasn't over. Now the states had to ratify the amendment.

According to the United States Constitution, three-fourths of the states, or thirty-six of the forty-eight, had to approve an amendment before it could become law.

Carrie Catt and Alice Paul feverishly campaigned, as did others, including black women. If the states acted quickly, women could vote in the 1920 presidential election. Otherwise they'd have to wait another four years!

A political cartoon shows a well-dressed father shocked that his daughter is campaigning for suffrage. The caption reads, "His daughter! And he thought she was 'just a little girl.'"

Catt and Paul telegraphed state governors for support, urging them to bring the amendment before a special legislative session. Some governors opposed the amendment and refused the suffragists' request. Others were reluctant to hold a special session because of the cost. So suffragists volunteered to handle clerical work without getting paid. At the end of 1919, the Nineteenth Amendment had been approved by twenty-two states.

In June 1920, the Republican and Democratic parties held their presidential conventions. The Republicans chose Sen. Warren G. Harding of Ohio as their candidate, and the Democrats selected Gov. James Cox of Ohio as theirs. Mary Church Terrell, president of the Women's Republican League of Washington, campaigned for Harding. The candidates welcomed the women as potential voters and supported the Nineteenth Amendment. By summer, thirty-five states had voted to ratify the amendment. However, several Southern states including Georgia, Alabama, Virginia, and North and South Carolina vehemently rejected the proposal. There was only one state left where a vote could be taken that year: Tennessee.

On August 9, legislators gathered in Nashville. Those in favor of suffrage wore yellow roses; those opposed wore red ones. Suffragists lobbied the senators to vote yes. Anti-suffragists tried to sway lawmakers with liquor and get them drunk the night before the vote. They threatened to financially ruin those who were for suffrage. Legislators in North Carolina had just defeated the amendment, and they urged Tennessee lawmakers to fight suffrage "to the last ditch, and then some."

Miss Josephine Pearson, President of the Tennessee Division of the Southern Women's League, leads a rally to reject the Nineteenth Amendment, August 1920.

On August 18, the amendment came to a vote in the Tennessee House of Representatives. One pro-suffrage legislator was brought from the hospital so that he could vote. Another, torn between staying home with his dying child or voting, leaped off a moving train to vote yes, then rushed home on a chartered train.

Harry T. Burn, age twenty-four, was the youngest member of the legislature. Burn was a Republican from an anti-suffrage district in the mountains, and he sported a red rose on his jacket. However, no one knew how he really stood on the issue. In his pocket he carried a letter from his mother. She had written, "Hurrah and vote for Suffrage and don't keep them in doubt." So when Burn's name was called and he was asked

Representative Harry T. Burn, 1919.

if he would ratify the amendment, he answered, "Aye." The measure passed!

Afterward, when asked why he had supported suffrage, he said, "I knew that a mother's advice is always safest for her boy to follow, and my mother wanted me to vote for ratification."

Anti-suffragists tried to discredit the Tennessee vote, but the state's supreme court approved it, and the governor signed the "certificate of ratification." The certificate reached the U.S. secretary of state in the early morning of August 26. He confirmed that the document was in order, and signed papers declaring that ratification of the Nineteenth Amendment was complete.

GOV. R. H. ROBERTS SIGNING TENNESSEE CERTIFICATE OF RATIFICATION

Governor A. H. Roberts signing the Tennessee certificate of ratification, August 26, 1920.

The next day in South St. Paul, Minnesota, a special election was held, and eighty women voted on a bond bill for improvements of waterworks. At 6:00 a.m. Miss Margaret Newburgh voted; she is reputed to be the first woman in the country to cast her ballot under the new federal law.

In the national election of 1920, women age twenty-one and older voted for president. Mary Church Terrell had gone to New York in September to work at the national Republican headquarters and organize black women in the East during the campaign. She had urged them to use their newly won franchise and vote for Harding. "We women have now a weapon of defense which we have never possessed before," she wrote. "It will be a shame and reproach to us if we do not use it. However much the white women of the country need suffrage, colored women need it more."

Harding won in a landslide victory. Twenty-seven million women celebrated their victory too, for they now had full voting rights. After a campaign lasting seventy-two years, women's voices were finally heard.

Yet for many women the battle was not over. Native American women (and men) couldn't vote until the Snyder Act of 1924 deemed them citizens, and even after that most still had to be granted voting rights state by state. Not until 1962

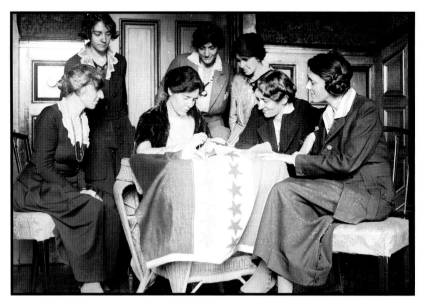

Every time a state ratified the Nineteenth Amendment, someone at headquarters sewed a new star on the party's suffrage flag. Alice Paul sewed the final star.

did every state allow Native American men and women to vote. Countless black, Asian, and Latina women were not able to exercise those rights until the Voting Rights Act was passed in 1965.

"Who has the right to vote is still being decided today," said Lynda Blackmon Lowery, the youngest marcher from Selma to Montgomery.

Alice Paul unfurls the suffrage flag from the balcony of the Woman's Party headquarters when Tennessee ratified the Nineteenth Amendment, August 18, 1920.

CHAPTER 10: HOW TO STEAL AN ELECTION

"Dead or alive, they would all cast a good vote."

—Testimony of anonymous witness in 1864 trial of those accused of recording ballots for four hundred patients in Jarvis Hospital in Baltimore

CORRUPTION AND INTIMIDATION WERE IMPEDIMENTS TO a fair voting system. Election Day violence was not unusual. Dating back to colonial times, candidates and their supporters had not only cheated at the polls, they had committed crimes to ensure victory. Could a voter ever be certain that his or her vote would be counted?

The earliest method of voting was voicing one's choice in public. A citizen would literally stand up and say who he was voting for or raise his hand. This made intimidation easy. Around Election Day, candidates plied voters with rum, wine, and beer to win their votes, or bribed them with food and money. Since only property owners could vote, candidates often bought "freeholds," or temporary land rights, from large landowners. They gave these rights to landless men, and returned the deeds to the real owners after the election. Sometimes corrupt candidates would even pay voters *not* to vote so that they could win a majority.

A painting by George Caleb Bingham in the 1850s shows an Election Day scene in Saline County, Missouri. A voter, standing on the steps of the courthouse, swears to a judge that he is qualified to vote and has not already voted, and announces his choice. Election clerks sitting behind the judge record the voter's name and selection. Meanwhile, the candidate tips his hat to the voter and hands out calling cards to make sure that everyone knows his name. In those days campaigning at the polls was allowed.

The County Election by George Caleb Bingham, 1851–52.

Later in the nineteenth century, paper ballots replaced voice voting. Voters brought to the polls printed "party tickets" that they had received from their political parties. Or they cut ballots out of the newspaper. Voters carried their ballots to a designated building and passed them through a window into the hands of an election judge. In Baltimore, Maryland, on Election Day in 1859, George Kyle, a merchant who was a Democrat, left home with a bundle of ballots. On his way to the polls a "ruffian" tried to snatch his ballots. Then someone clobbered the merchant. "I felt a pistol put to my head," he said, and a bullet grazed him. "A man carrying a musket rushed at him. Another threw a brick, knocking him off his feet." The merchant picked himself up and ran but never cast his vote or delivered the ballots. The Democratic candidate for Congress lost, but he contested the election results. Three months later the House of Representatives looked into the crime committed against the merchant and decided that any "man of ordinary courage" could have made it to the polls. Baltimore was not unique. From 1850 to 1860, eighty-nine Americans were killed at the polls during Election Day riots.

At first voters had to write down the names of their choices. Sometimes they misspelled the names, and the votes were disqualified. So then the ballots were printed with colors and shapes to identify the candidates. Bankers, landlords, and powerful officials kept a close eye on the ballots. A "wrong vote" could mean the loss of a job or being denied a bank loan.

In many cities criminals controlled voting. One infamous example was Tammany Hall. William M. "Boss" Tweed, a corrupt city alderman, ruled a gang based at Tammany Hall in New York. Tweed's thugs used all kinds of tricks at the polls. They rounded up immigrants, rushed them to Democratic party headquarters, and filled out their applications for citizenship. Then they coached them on how to answer questions from the judge, and quickly had them naturalized so that they could vote. As many as eight hundred immigrants appeared before the judge in one day. Tweed later admitted, "I don't think there was ever a fair and honest election in New York City."

Tweed's gangs also intimidated voters by keeping them away from the polls. They hired "rowdies" to go into certain precincts on Election Day and start

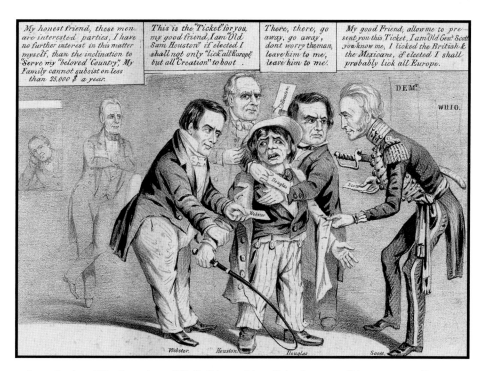

A cynical political cartoon "Soliciting a Vote" depicts candidates struggling to force their own election ticket on an "uncouth"-looking working man, New York 1852. In the left background, President Millard Fillmore looks in through a window, observing.

A political cartoon in *Harper's Weekly* shows Boss Tweed leaning defiantly at the ballot box with the caption, "As long as I count the Votes, what are you going to do about it? Say?"

fights and beat up prospective voters. And they imported prisoners from the penitentiary, and paupers from the poorhouse, and gave them clean clothes and money in return for voting for Tammany candidates. On Election Day, the gangs stuffed ballot boxes with phony ballots. In an 1844 election, fifty-five thousand votes were recorded in New York City. However, only forty-one thousand men were qualified to vote. "Observers commented that the city's dogs and cats must have been affected by an unusual dose of civic pride." Another scheme was to bring in voters from other areas, supposedly to lay pipe for the city's water supply. These illegal voters called "pipe-layers" went home after the election.

On the West Coast, in San Francisco, voters put their ballots into boxes. Some boxes contained secret compartments. Corrupt judges slid open the compartment doors, deposited fake ballots, and hid the real ones. Hired thugs smashed the metal boxes so often that the city used steel boilers instead to contain the ballots.

Newspapers printed accounts of election fraud. The *Baltimore Sun* published an editorial noting that Election Day violence had become too common. In many places armed gangs were imported to "regulate" elections. There seemed to be little that could be done about the flagrant fraud.

On the Wabash River in Illinois, voters were ferried into towns to vote more than once, and were called "repeaters." Representative Abraham Lincoln condemned the illegal voters at a session of the Illinois state legislature. He proposed punishment for "those who could abuse such a right." But no voting laws were passed. Local elections were easier to corrupt than state elections, but even presidential elections offered opportunities for crookedness.

In 1860, the Republicans chose Abraham Lincoln as their candidate for president. At that time, the nation was bitterly divided on the issue of slavery. Lincoln, a moderate, opposed slavery. His views infuriated Southern slave-holders. So they threw their support to the Democratic candidate, John C. Breckinridge of Kentucky. To make sure their candidate won, ten states in the South took Lincoln's name off the ballot. In parts of the North, voters also preferred the Democrats. Tammany Hall tried to rig the election by registering the names of five hundred dead people to vote for Breckinridge. Four hundred patients in a Baltimore hospital who couldn't get to the polls were also recorded as having voted. "Dead or alive, they would all cast a good vote," said a witness at a voting fraud court case later.

In Albany, New York, a Democratic election inspector appointed a group of butchers as "special constables" to patrol the polls. The butchers formed a wedge and wouldn't let Republicans cast their votes. The tickets bore the marks and colors of the party, and if a Republican tried to conceal his ballot inside a Democratic ticket and the butchers found out, they chased him away so that he couldn't vote at all.

Despite all these shenanigans, Lincoln won the popular vote as well as the Electoral College vote.

Shortly after Lincoln's inauguration the Civil War broke out, and new voting problems arose during the war years. Usually voters were required to show residency. But what about soldiers who were fighting away from home? Could they cast their ballots to select members of Congress, for example? Congress decided how much money to spend on the military, and whether or not to impeach a president. Shouldn't men fighting for their country have a say in these matters? The issue was fiercely debated.

In 1862, Wisconsin became the first state to permit soldiers to vote in the field. Eventually nineteen states passed laws allowing soldiers to vote by absentee ballot. However, those new laws presented perfect occasions for fraud. Officers who distributed and counted the ballots could falsify the numbers. To protect the votes, Iowa appointed election commissioners for each regiment. Connecticut went even further and excluded officers from election duties. Instead, it appointed civilian monitors.

Indiana did not yet allow soldiers

Abraham Lincoln campaign button for the 1864 presidential election.

in the field to vote during an election for governor in October 1864. But troops from the 60th Massachusetts Regiment, who were stationed in Indianapolis, voted a dozen times each. Some soldiers boasted that they voted twenty-five times!

In the 1864 presidential election, Lincoln ran again and won easily. But the worst violence around voting occurred after the Civil War ended. The Thirteenth Amendment, abolishing slavery in the United States, was ratified in December 1865. Southern states retaliated by passing Jim Crow laws to segregate black people and prevent black men from voting by imposing poll taxes and unfair tests.

Of course, the greatest impediment to a fair voting system was to simply withhold the right to vote. In the Southwestern states, Mexican and other Spanish-speaking people faced the same kind of discrimination as African Americans. When the Mexican-American War had ended in 1848, the people living in the territories ceded from Mexico—in areas now included in the states of New Mexico, Utah, Nevada, Arizona, California, Texas, and western Colorado—had the opportunity to become American citizens. But their status was second-class. White settlers and landowners insulted them and controlled their political lives. Spanish-speaking people, valuing their own culture and traditions, retreated into separate communities called barrios.

Many new immigrants from Mexico worked in the fields of Texas, California, and Arizona as farm laborers. Their poverty prevented them from paying unfair poll taxes. What's more, voting forms and literacy tests written in English made voting impossible. When Latinos signed their ballots with an X instead of a signature, the ballots were thrown out. And sometimes farmworkers couldn't even get to the polls because their hours had been intentionally shortened. In the twentieth century, Spanish-speaking citizens across the Southwest became America's "forgotten minority." The vote was not available to *all* Mexican Americans until 1975, when amendments to the Voting Rights Act forced state governments to make changes to their voting procedures, including providing ballots in languages other than English.

Chinese immigrants endured bigotry too. They had come to California in 1848 to mine for gold, and then to build the transcontinental railroad. A law passed in 1790 prohibited Chinese people, mostly men in those years, from becoming citizens. They were not allowed to vote, marry white women, or testify in court. Barred from many occupations, they took low-paying jobs as farm laborers, servants, cooks, and laundrymen.

In 1876, race hatred escalated and politicians demanded that Chinese immigrants be kicked out of the United States. "Chinese must go!" was the rallying cry. New discriminatory laws were passed, culminating in the Chinese Exclusion Act of 1882. This was the first time the United States had excluded immigrants because of their nationality or race.

For the next twenty years, as the law was renewed, Chinese were not allowed to enter the country, much less vote. Under the terms of this act, immigrants from China who remained in the country could not become citizens and were forced to live apart. Chinatowns sprang up from California to Connecticut, with district associations providing services that should have come from the government. It was not until 1943 that Congress repealed the exclusion laws and granted citizenship to Chinese Americans.

Other people of Asian ancestry also were prevented from becoming citizens and voting. In 1922 the Supreme Court ruled, in *Ozawa v. United States*, that people of Japanese heritage could not become citizens. Then in 1923, in *United States v. Bhagat Singh Thind*, the Supreme Court decreed that people of Asian Indian and other Asian ancestries could not become citizens. It wasn't until 1953, when the McCarran-Walter Act was passed by Congress, that all people of Asian ancestry become eligible for citizenship and finally won the right to vote!

CHAPTER 11: THE SECRET BALLOT

"All elections require money. You can't have an election without it."

—Fred R. Bishop, treasurer of the Democratic campaign fund, Louisville, Kentucky

WINNING THE RIGHT TO VOTE WAS ONE THING—ACTUALLY exercising it was another thing entirely. After the Civil War, formerly enslaved black men were free and entitled to vote. The Fifteenth Amendment, ratified in 1870, guaranteed that right. However, Southern white Democrats blocked black men from voting by using terror. The Ku Klux Klan was born, and members showed up on Election Day. Freedmen attempting to vote would be whipped, shot at, and threatened with death. The KKK issued a warning to black men: "Beware! Your steps are marked! The eye of the dark chief is upon you. First he warns; then the avenging dagger flashes in the moonlight."

A political cartoon in *Harper's Weekly* showed an African American lying dead with a bullet wound in his head because he had dared to go to the polls. In the presidential election of 1868, Republican candidate Ulysses S. Grant, the former commander of the Union Army, did not receive a single vote in St. Landry Parish, Louisiana. The registration supervisor was not surprised. He said, "I am fully convinced that no man could have voted any other than the Democratic ticket and not been killed inside of twenty-four hours." Grant received only one vote in Bossier Parish, Louisiana, although two thousand Republicans were registered. Throughout Louisiana, state workers were threatened with losing their jobs if they did not vote for the Democratic candidate. A committee in New Orleans deplored the violence. Yet an anonymous member of the White League said: "It has been charged that the white man's party intends to achieve success by intimidation. This is strictly true."

COPYRIGHT—1923.
THE HAMMOND STUDIOS,
MERIDIAN, AND JACKSON, MISS

Ku Klux Klan initiation in Meridian and Jackson, Mississippi, 1923.

New laws in Mississippi gave total power to local white registrars, who determined whether applicants passed a literacy test and could register to vote. Throughout the South the laws were disastrous for black people, even those who were eligible to vote. The situation was almost as bad in the North. What could be done to reform the voting process?

Outraged citizens demanded change. Committees held meetings in New York to challenge election fraud. But they had no success with city courts and state party leaders. So committee members asked Congress for a "uniform election law" that would guarantee the "free right of voting." The Republicans responded by introducing the Enforcement Acts, which prohibited intimidation and violence at the polls. The acts also forbade racially biased election laws such as poll taxes and literacy tests. Election supervisors were appointed to watch for irregularities in enforcing the new laws. They found plenty of violators. Supervisors brought seven hundred cases before the Justice Department each year.

But election fraud continued. In the presidential election of 1876, Gov. Rutherford Hayes of Ohio, a Republican, ran against New York's Gov. Samuel Tilden. In New York City, Tammany registered thousands of fictitious names to vote for Tilden. Big Tim Sullivan, a prominent Tammany leader, devised another scheme. On Election Day he brought in "repeaters," men who had full beards. "When you've voted them with their whiskers on," said Sullivan, "you take them to a barber and scrape off the chin fringe." The repeaters then voted a second time. Next, barbers shaved more of the men's facial hair, leaving only their moustaches, and they voted again. "If that ain't enough and the box can stand a few more ballots," boasted Sullivan, "clean off the moustache and vote them plain face. That makes one of them good for four votes."

When Hayes won the election, people questioned his victory. Congress set up a special commission to investigate. An editorial in *The Nation* read, "No honorable man could accept the Presidency if before accepting it he was bound

Dr. H. W. Evans, Imperial Wizard of the Ku Klux Klan, leading his Knights of the Klan in the parade held in Washington, D.C., 1925.

to satisfy himself that in every state in which he had a majority, the vote has been lawfully cast and the count honestly made." Two days before the inauguration, the commission announced that Hayes was the winner. However, historians believe that the Republicans struck a deal with the Southern Democrats to make it happen.

Then a new idea came along: the secret ballot. The system had begun in Australia. The state government would print a ballot containing the names of all the party nominees. Voters would privately mark their choices in booths or rooms divided into compartments, and put their ballots into boxes. This is how we vote today.

"If the act of voting were performed in secret," predicted *The Nation*, "no bribed voter could or would be trusted to carry out his bargain when left to himself." The first state to adopt the method was Massachusetts, and all but three states followed by the early 1900s.

But new problems arose. Since the states printed the ballots, they could decide whether or not to include third-party candidates. And most states didn't. In Louisiana, for example, a newspaper announced, "It is the religious duty of Democrats to rob Populists and Republicans of their votes whenever and wherever the opportunity presents itself." The Populists were an alliance of farmers and working-class people in the West, Midwest, and South. During this period of rapid industrial growth, the Populists advocated tax reforms, pensions, and aid from the federal government in hard times.

In Robertson County, Texas, in 1896, Democrats actually stole ballot boxes on Election Day because some of the candidates were African Americans. To make sure that the Democratic county judge won, Democrats paraded around black precincts with their pistols raised and scared thousands of voters away from the polls.

In Louisville, Kentucky, Democrats bought elections. Candidates for various offices were forced to contribute a percentage of their salaries to the campaign fund. "All elections require money," claimed Fred R. Bishop, the treasurer of the Democratic campaign fund. "You can't have an election without it." The money wasn't used for buttons or posters. Instead, it went to bribe the captain of a district or ward. The captain assigned policemen and firemen to register "phantom" voters on Election Day.

The third-party challengers, the Fusionists, were told that they couldn't vote because there weren't enough ballots. The Fusionist Party combined black Republicans and white Populists. Since some of these voters couldn't read or write, the Fusionists added symbols to the ballots to help party members cast their votes. In a precinct of the Third Ward in Louisville, armed men took the ballot box at gunpoint and carried it away. The 1905 election for mayor in Louisville was so corrupt that the Fusionists raised funds to contest the results. In March 1907 the court ruled on the election and concluded that although there had been fraud, not enough ballots had been stolen to affect the outcome of the election. "Many of the Democrats behaved very badly," concluded the judges, "but the place to deal with them is in the criminal and not in the civil courts."

But when the case went to the court of appeals, the judges agreed with the Fusionists and overturned the previous ruling. A "free and fair" election had *not* been held. Therefore the mayor and other city officials who had won in the 1905 election were ordered to immediately vacate their offices, and a new election was scheduled for November. The *Evening Post* proclaimed the ruling a "triumph of democracy."

Would voting at last become honest and fair in the twentieth century? If women gained the right to vote, could they bring about change?

CHAPTER 12: BULLYING AT THE BALLOT BOX

"One person, one vote."

—William O. Douglas (1898–1980), associate justice
of the U.S. Supreme Court

WOMEN HAD BEEN OBSERVING CROOKED ELECTIONS FOR years. As they struggled to win the vote, some states foiled their efforts by not presenting their amendment on the ballot. Some local and city politicians who wanted to control election outcomes did not support women's suffrage because a larger number of voters would be harder to manipulate.

In Wisconsin and North Dakota, for example, the ballots for a vote on suffrage were a different size and color that could easily be spotted and thrown away. In a 1919 Texas suffrage election, a male supporter warned the suffragists: "The counting is what counts and gets results.. . . Just count and count some more and you will be sure to win." But the amendment failed that year. Polls in some districts of Texas that supported women's suffrage never opened on Election Day.

Yet in 1920 when women finally did win the right to vote, would they make a difference? What could they do to make elections fair? Could they even put a woman in office? As early as 1916, four years before the Nineteenth Amendment was passed and ratified, Jeanette Rankin of Montana, a social worker and lobbyist for the NAWSA, won an election for the House of Representatives. Rankin said, "I may be the first woman member of Congress but I won't be the last." Montana had given women the right to vote in 1914, because of Rankin's efforts. She felt that if women could vote, they would make laws that were kinder and more likely to address the needs of everyday people. When she ran for Congress, she drove from place to place making speeches at town halls and factories, visiting farmers, leading a parade at the state fair, and meeting with political leaders to ask for their support.

Minutes after she walked into the House of Representatives for the first time, in April 1917, President Wilson asked Congress to declare war on Germany and fight on the side of Great Britain and France. For the next three days Congress debated the issue. Rankin was a pacifist and opposed war. Her suffragist friends tried to pressure her into making decisions that reflected their views. Alice Paul, a fellow pacifist, wanted

Congresswoman Jeannette Rankin on her first day at the Capital, in 1917, holds a bouquet of purple and yellow flowers, the colors of the Congressional Union, a suffragist group that opposed the war.

Rankin to vote against war. But Carrie Catt urged her to agree to a declaration of war. A yes vote would show that women were strong and patriotic, Catt reasoned. Finally, when the vote was taken, Rankin said, "I want to stand for my country, but I cannot vote for war."

Catt was angry with her and said, "Miss Rankin was not voting for the suffragists of the nation; she represents Montana." Yet years later Rankin said, "I believe that the first vote I cast was the most significant vote and a most significant act on the part of women, because women are going to have to stop war." In 1918 Rankin helped found and headed a Committee on Woman Suffrage and worked to win the vote for all American women. When the House of Representatives debated the issue of a constitutional amendment for women's right to vote, she was the first to speak. After the Nineteenth Amendment was passed, she dedicated herself to lobbying for laws that would improve the lives of workers, families, and children.

Congresswoman Jeannette Rankin of Montana gives a speech from the National American Woman Suffrage Association (NAWSA) headquarters in Washington, D.C. Carrie Chapman Catt, president of NAWSA, stands behind her.

Carrie Catt, the former leader of the NAWSA, transformed her organization into the League of Women Voters. The league worked to bring out the vote and educate women who had never voted before about their new responsibilities. As women joined the ranks of voters, however, they tended to vote for the same parties and candidates as their husbands, fathers, and brothers.

Meanwhile, political reformers figured the way to make elections fair was to introduce a new method of voting: the machine. First came the punch-card machine, then one with a lever. In the early twentieth century many states used voting machines on Election Day. But there were still problems. How could voters add write-in candidates? Also, how could a voter split the ticket? A voter might want a Republican candidate for one office, but a Democrat for another. No one could be sure that a vote was accurately recorded. And the machines often broke down. Or they were broken on purpose. A person could stick a piece of pencil lead into the gears of a lever machine and votes wouldn't be counted.

So in 1908 New Jersey returned to paper ballots. Today most states use a combination of paper ballots that can be used as backup and electronic

Huey P. Long, the "Kingfish," served in the U.S. Senate for three years, and angered his fellow senators who called him a troublemaker. Long was accustomed to charges of election fraud such as handpicking candidates and putting fake "dummy" candidates on the ballot.

technology that makes counting votes easier and faster. Oregon conducts all elections by mail. Voters simply send in their ballots. However, with this system, days before an election candidates can see lists of those who have not yet voted, and ply them with campaign materials to try to win them over.

Despite efforts to reform voting, the "culture of corruption" flourished in the twentieth century. Sen. Huey P. Long, nicknamed the "Kingfish," ruled Louisiana like a dictator. He had the names of legal voters scratched from the registry rolls. Long even summoned the National Guard to stand by with machine guns as ballot boxes were opened in his hotel suite and he "oversaw" the counting. But not everyone was willing to be bullied.

The women's division of Louisiana's Honest Election League worked to defeat Long's corrupt methods. They investigated how election commissioners were appointed, and hired attorneys to train hundreds of women in election law. Some of them became election commissioners themselves. The league removed thousands of false names from the New Orleans voting rolls, and monitored the polls. In 1940, a group of young law students headed by Corinne "Lindy" Boggs, who later became a congresswoman, went door to door verifying registration lists. Long's men harassed Boggs's group, and tried to frighten them with vicious dogs. Nevertheless, the women forged on, canvassing precincts and challenging fraudulent voters. However, "their actions made little headway against the powerful forces" of Long and his cohorts, according to historians. Some women hesitated to cast votes because "the simple act of placing a paper ballot into a wooden box could be accompanied by taunts, jeers, threats, or even fisticuffs."

What could be done?

Some people turned to the courts. Cases concerning voting rights came before the Supreme Court. One case in 1962 pertained to an imbalance of voting power in Georgia. The state divided districts unfairly. A rural county had fewer people than a more populated urban area. Yet the rural county had a greater percentage of the vote in the Electoral College. Associate Justice William O. Douglas handed down the court's majority decision forcing the states to redraw the districts. He wrote: "The conception of political equality from the Declaration of Independence, to Lincoln's Gettysburg Address, to the Fifteenth, Seventeenth, and Nineteenth Amendments can mean only one thing—one person, one vote."

That year a young member of the school board in Plains, Georgia, ran for state senator. His name was Jimmy Carter. Carter heard that voting procedures in Quitman County were rigged by a typical cigar-smoking boss, so he sent an aide to see if the stories were true. Sure enough, the boss had moved the polling booth out of the courthouse and into the office of a local judge. The boss had then hung around the polls, telling people to vote for Carter's opponent. When one couple slipped their ballots into the box, the boss took them out and tore them up, telling the couple, "You haven't learned anything about voting my way." Then he gave the couple new ballots that were already marked for Carter's opponent. "That's the way you're supposed to vote," he said. "I have been running my county my way for twenty years."

Carter lost, but he protested. Newspaper reporters said to him, "Mr. Carter, everybody knows it's not right but this is the way they always run elections over here." So Carter decided to contest the election. "I had been betrayed by a political system in which I had had confidence," he said, "and I was mad as hell."

John Pennington, a reporter for the *Atlanta Journal*, felt angry too, and exposed fraudulent voting practices in Quitman County. He found evidence of false registrations, including a man who had died the previous summer yet was listed as having voted, and a prisoner in the penitentiary who was also listed as a voter. Armed with evidence, Carter took his case before the Quitman County Democratic Party executive committee. When the committee refused to hear his complaint, Carter and his legal team appeared before a Democratic recount committee. The judge ordered the ballot box to be opened in his court. Flaps on the ballots were not sealed. Ballot stubs were missing, making it impossible to identify illegal voters or to determine the total number of those certified to vote. The judge declared the election invalid.

A few years later Jimmy Carter was elected governor of Georgia. His wife, Rosalynn, did not follow the accustomed passive role of most wives of politicians. She campaigned for her husband, which was unusual at that time. When he ran for president she hit the campaign trail again, and gave speeches in forty-two states. Many people outside of Georgia didn't know Carter. Rosalynn introduced herself and said, "My husband's running for president."

"President of what?" they asked.

"President of the United States," she answered.

People were astonished. They had never met a presidential candidate's wife before. "You've got to be kidding. Is this an election year?"

In 1977, Carter was elected President of the United States. He regarded himself as a new kind of Southerner, opposed to racial discrimination. And Rosalynn was a new kind of First Lady, sitting in on cabinet meetings to be well informed, and working for human rights. Unlike President Wilson's wives, who had stayed out of politics and had not even supported the Nineteenth Amendment, Rosalynn worked alongside her husband. She and the president supported the Equal Rights Amendment (ERA), guaranteeing women legal protection under the Constitution.

Many laws, especially state laws, had separate provisions for women that were unfair. In some states women needed to have their husbands' consent before selling property. In Alabama, girls had to be seventeen before they could be newspaper carriers, but boys only had to be ten. The ERA had been introduced by suffragist Alice Paul back in 1923, and had been passed by Congress in 1972. The amendment still needed to be ratified by the required number of states. Rosalynn made speeches and attended meetings to win support for the amendment. She later said her greatest disappointment as First Lady was the failure of the ERA to be ratified.

Nonetheless, progress was finally being made. The Carters had found that "fair and free" elections were a good way to resolve or prevent armed conflicts.

CHAPTER 13: BREAKING BARRIERS

"Old enough to fight, old enough to vote."

—Franklin D. Roosevelt (1882–1945), thirty-second president
of the United States

GEORGIA WAS THE FIRST STATE TO INITIATE A CHANGE IN voting rights that affected young adults. In 1943, the legislature passed a measure to lower the voting age from twenty-one to eighteen in state and local elections. "Fight at 18, vote at 18" was the slogan for this state's reform effort.

The campaign for lowering the voting age had begun during World War II when President Franklin D. Roosevelt changed the draft age from twenty-one to eighteen. The campaign's motto was "Old enough to fight, old enough to vote." Many people thought that teenagers sent to war should have a say in their government's decisions.

The amendment received support from the National Education Association. The association pointed out that a greater number of young adults were graduating from high school than had in years past, and that they would be informed citizens.

However, the proposal for the amendment failed to pass in Congress. But when Gen. Dwight D. Eisenhower became president in 1953, he pushed for the amendment, perhaps because of his own military background. Echoing President Franklin D. Roosevelt's sentiments, he said, "If a man is old enough to fight, he is old enough to vote." Many Democrats and Republicans supported the proposal because they would gain more voters. Others disagreed. Congressman Emanuel Celler, a New York Democrat, said, "To my mind the draft age and the voting age are as different as chalk is from cheese." He believed that the years from age eighteen to twenty-one were "years of rebellion rather than reflection." Fun-loving teenagers were incapable of making good choices, he thought. Many people agreed with him. Even those who didn't thought that the voting age was a state matter rather than a federal one.

Everything changed during the Vietnam War. In 1954, Vietnam was divided into northern and southern zones at the Geneva Conference. The north attempted to put the whole country under Communist leadership. The United States sent military advisers to South Vietnam because it wanted to block the spread of Communism in Asia. Then, in 1965, American combat troops were sent.

For the first time, Americans viewed war on national television, and they were horrified by the atrocities. They were aghast to see how the war was demoralizing young soldiers. The compulsory draft age for Americans was eighteen. Each month young men were being conscripted into the armed forces. As the war dragged on, casualties increased. Most of the soldiers killed were only eighteen and nineteen. The monthly draft call rose from seventeen thousand to thirty-five thousand in 1966.

Students protesting the Vietnam War march at the University of Wisconsin-Madison in 1966.

Courtesy of the University of Wisconsin-Madison Archives (ID S00673).

Many young draftees purposely injured themselves to fail the physical, or pretended to be mentally unfit. Some young men burned their draft cards. Others fled to Canada or Sweden. The controversial war triggered a reconsideration of the voting-age amendment. To many it seemed undemocratic to send teenagers into war without giving them the vote.

Groups such as Let Us Vote, the NAACP, and the National Student Association lobbied in support of the amendment. The *New York Times* wrote in an editorial, "Young people . . . are far better prepared educationally for the voting privilege than the bulk of the nation's voters have been through much of its history." College students across the country were more politically active than ever before. They vehemently protested the Vietnam War and held rallies.

On Friday, May 1, 1970, students at Kent State University in Ohio organized an antiwar demonstration that continued over the weekend. Alarmed, Mayor LeRoy Satrom called in the National Guard. A rally scheduled for Monday at noon was banned. Nevertheless, angry students gathered on the campus.

When a police officer ordered the students to disperse, they refused. Instead, the kids yelled and hurled rocks. Guardsmen threw tear gas canisters into the crowd. Students marched over a hill and onto a practice football field. All of a sudden guardsmen fired their rifles and pistols. Sandra Scheuer and William Schroeder were fatally struck by the gunfire on their way to class. Allison Krause, age nineteen, was shot and killed. Jeffrey Miller was shot in the mouth. Mary Ann Vecchio, a fourteen-year-old who had run away from home to join the anti-war effort, screamed for help as she knelt beside Miller's dead body. John Filo, a photography student, snapped a picture of her that appeared on the front pages of newspapers throughout the country the next day and became an iconic image of the era.

The shooting at Kent State spurred legislators into action. Sen. Edward Kennedy added a proposal for lowering the voting age to an amendment to the Voting Rights Act of 1965. After a brief debate, the Senate approved it. On June 20, 1970, President Richard Nixon reluctantly signed the bill. He wasn't sure that the voting-age clause was constitutional, and urged the attorney general to swiftly test the bill in the courts. Meanwhile, support for the amendment grew nationally.

Mary Ann Vecchio kneels over the body of student Jeffrey Miller, shot by Ohio National Guard troops during an anti-war demonstration at Kent State University, May 4, 1970.

However, not everyone had been won over to the idea. Texas and Oregon sued Attorney General John Mitchell to prevent him from enforcing the new law in their states. Arizona and Idaho refused to implement the law, and the United States sued to force them to follow it. The cases were combined as *Oregon v. Mitchell*, and came before the Supreme Court in December 1970. The lawyers for Texas and Oregon argued that the amendment took away the states' power to set their own voting requirements. The justices disagreed. With a one-vote majority they ruled that lowering the voting age to eighteen in federal elections was constitutional. Justice William O. Douglas handed down the court's opinion. "Those who have such a large 'stake' in modern elections as 18-year-olds, whether in times of war or peace, should have political equality."

The Court did not rule on state and local elections, though, so in some states a teenager could vote for president and vice president but not for state officials. It seemed unfair to say a young person was old enough to vote for those who ran the country, but too young to have a say in local issues. So Congress adopted a constitutional amendment setting the national voting age at eighteen in *all* elections.

In March 1971, the proposal was adopted by both houses of Congress and sent to the states for ratification. By the end of June, thirty-eight states—the necessary number—had ratified the Twenty-Sixth Amendment. It stated that the right to vote could not be denied to "citizens of the United States who are eighteen years of age or older." This amendment was the quickest to be ratified in the history of the United States. On July 1, 1971, the new law became part of the Constitution. At a White House ceremony President Nixon said that he believed "young Americans" would "infuse into this country some idealism, some courage, some stamina, some high moral strength."

Would eighteen- and nineteen-year-olds live up to the president's vision of them and make the most of their privilege?

CHAPTER 14: YOUNG VOTING VOICES

"We're voting and we matter."

—Daniel Hernandez Jr. (1991–), member of the Arizona
House of Representatives

FOLLOWING IN THE TRADITION OF THE BIRMINGHAM Children's Crusade back in 1963, young people are standing up for their rights as potential voters. Teenagers still in high school want to have a say in matters and laws that apply to them.

Daniel Hernandez Jr. was a seventeen-year-old high school senior in Tucson, Arizona, when he volunteered to work for the 2008 presidential campaign

Daniel Hernandez Jr., a Democrat, is a member of the Arizona House of Representatives from the 2nd district. He was elected to office in 2016.

of Hillary Clinton, then a senator from New York. She hoped to capture the Democratic nomination.

"It was very strange that we had only had male presidents," said Daniel. "Why never a woman? I grew up surrounded by strong women—my mother and two sisters." Daniel turned eighteen in January 2009 and voted in the primary.

"A lot of times people who don't look like me are in office," said Daniel. As he became involved in politics, his father and some of their neighbors caught his enthusiasm and started voting for the first time in twenty years. "We're voting and we matter," Daniel said.

Andrew Rubin voted for the first time in 2000, when he was eighteen and an urban planning major at Cal Poly San Luis Obispo in California. Former Texas governor George Bush was running against Vice President Al Gore. "Gore was very dedicated to the issue of environmental change," said Andrew. Gore, ahead of his time, made this a central pillar of his campaign, stressing the sensitivity of the earth's climate and global warming caused by human activities. His platform focused on strong measures to protect the environment.

Gore had the most popular votes, but Bush won the Electoral College by a narrow margin. Although Gore lost the election, the problem of global warming did not go away. Glaciers are melting. Sea levels are rising. A group of teenagers recently formed a national movement, Zero Hour, to call for action on climate change. They say this is the greatest crisis threatening their generation. Jamie Margolin, who was only sixteen when she founded the group, is now able to vote and influence lawmakers.

Jamie Margolin in 2018 when she founded the Zero Hour movement to raise awareness of climate justice issues. Dozens of environmental advocacy groups have sponsored her cause.

Jake Kolpas, an elementary school teacher in San Francisco, voted for the first time by absentee ballot in 2008 while he was at Hampshire College in Massachusetts. "I voted for Barack

Obama," said Jake. "He was a candidate whose views aligned with mine. And Obama won! Our first black president!"

In the 2016 primary, Jake supported Bernie Sanders, an independent and self-described Democratic Socialist candidate who later joined the Democratic Party. Sanders, a congressman from Vermont, was running against Hillary Clinton for the Democratic nomination. Jake said, "People in my age group thought Sanders was dependable and trustworthy." Thousands of young adults supported the seventy-four-year-old candidate.

"I really like his [Sanders'] point of view," said Angelica Collado, a Queens College student in New York, as she was about to vote. "And I think he'll continue what Obama has really started." Faced with college debt and a lack of good jobs, young people cheered Sanders' promises of free tuition for state universities and colleges.

However, Hillary Clinton won the primary and became the Democratic candidate for president. She ran against television star and real estate mogul Donald Trump, the Republican candidate. To the surprise of many Americans, Trump won the Electoral College vote, although Clinton was leading up till the last minute and won the popular vote. Some critics said that television won the election because Trump had produced and starred in *The Apprentice*, a popular reality TV show that reached a mass audience. However, many took offense at comments he made that they considered racist or misogynist.

His win threw the country into an uproar. The *New York Times* reported that Russian hackers had meddled in the election and had acted to aid Trump. Charges of voting fraud were heard once again. Although the Russians obviously hadn't stolen ballot boxes at gunpoint, or scared away voters from the polls, they were accused of spreading "fake news" reports about Clinton through social media and tipping the election. Were the accusations true?

President Trump claimed that illegal voting had cost him the popular vote. He demanded personal information for two hundred million voters to see if they were active and registered. At the time of this writing, election officials from both parties are investigating the 2016 presidential election. However, there is little doubt that Russia succeeded in stirring up doubts in the minds of some American voters.

A scandal broke in early 2018 when the *New York Times* and London's

Observer revealed that Trump's election campaign had hired Cambridge Analytica, a political consulting firm, to gain private information on more than fifty million Facebook users. Data about the personality traits of American voters and what they liked had been taken illegally from a survey for the purpose of targeting digital ads. People who had participated in the survey believed it was for academic reasons. Facebook CEO Mark Zuckerberg apologized for the mistake in a letter published in newspapers on March 25, 2018, but the damage had already been done. Young voters who used Facebook may have unwittingly contributed details to Cambridge Analytica and been influenced by the campaign ads.

Wes Davis, a second-year student at Texas A&M University who is majoring in political science, voted for Trump. Yet he says: "It's hard to overlook that Russians helped him [Trump] get elected. He was never my first choice. I would rather have had Jeb Bush, an honest and nice guy who embraces the history of this nation."

Wes, a registered Republican and a conservative, based his vote on the economy: business, taxes, and government regulations. "Our economy is in a good spot," he said. "With a strong economy everything else will fall in line."

When asked if he would vote for Trump again in 2020, Wes said: "I'd like another Republican challenger to try. He [Trump] does a lot of things to make the White House look dumb."

Others disagree. In a letter to the *New York Times*, Jason Peck of Holtsville, New York, wrote: "President Trump has exceeded my wildest expectations. . . . If it takes putting up with Mr. Trump's brash ways to see things get done, that is a deal I'm willing to accept."

Emily Robertson of Austin, Texas, wrote to the *New York Times*, "I'm thrilled with the progress that President Trump has made in defeating ISIS, cutting taxes for middle-class families, and making court appointments."

Some young people are not so thrilled, and are getting involved in politics as a reaction to President Trump's victory. Tahseen Chowdhury, a Democrat and a high school senior, planned to run for a New York State Senate seat in Queens, the borough Trump originally comes from. Tahseen turned eighteen just in time for the 2018 primary and a chance to vote for himself. He said, "The fact that I'm a teenager is very key. I have no interest in advocating for anyone other than my community."

Later he withdrew from the race because he felt he had accomplished his goal of joining his grassroots movement with mainline Democrats.

In Kansas, where there is no minimum age for governor's races, two sixteen-year-olds announced that they would seek the Democratic nomination for governor. And a seventeen-year-old declared that he would run as a Republican candidate.

Will Haskell of Westport, Connecticut, began his campaign for the Senate before graduating from college. He had planned to attend law school but changed his mind. "I woke up after Trump's election," said Will, age twenty-two in 2018, "and like a lot of other people felt like I had to get involved in the fight against Trump's agenda. That fight starts at the local and state level."

Will, a Democrat, disagreed with the voting record of Republican Sen. Toni Boucher, age sixty-eight, on issues such as gun control and voting rights. Will sent emails to his supporters showing how he would vote differently. His campaign manager was his college roommate from Georgetown University, and many of his campaign volunteers were high school students.

Even teenagers too young to vote can canvass neighborhoods and learn about elections. Like the kids in Alabama who marched to fight for their parents' right to vote, teenagers are participating, and launching crusades such as Zero Hour to address issues that will impact their future. Jamie Margolin, the founder of the movement, says, "We're going to change history."

CHAPTER 15: THE PRECIOUS RIGHT TO VOTE

"At the ages of eight and ten, we may have been too young to vote, but you are never too young to fight for what is right."

—Sheyann Webb (1956–), civil rights activist who marched for voting rights in Selma, Alabama, when she was only eight

DESPITE SETBACKS AFTER THE 2016 ELECTION, MANY AFRICAN Americans were determined to keep taking part in the political process. Stacy White, a computer science professor at Mississippi Valley State College, said: "I still feel positive. If I don't vote my voice is not heard."

She registered to vote on the day of her eighteenth birthday. "My parents explained to my fraternal twin sister, Marsha, and me that we were the legal age to vote and for us to go to the courthouse to register. This was their present to us," said Stacy. "I had just graduated from high school the previous May and was entering my freshman year that fall at the University of Mississippi."

"I was so very proud to register to vote on my eighteenth birthday because I knew the sacrifices that had been made by others for the privileges that I was provided. So many African Americans had been refused the right to vote. Some were killed, denied jobs, blacklisted, harassed, and their homes and churches firebombed. I didn't take my voting rights for granted."

Stacy's mother, a college-educated science teacher, had first tried to register to vote in Sunflower County, Mississippi, in 1956. The circuit clerk said to her, "Come back in March." Mrs. White went back in March and the clerk said, "We're not voting here. Go down to City Hall." She and her husband returned again and again to register, but were turned down each time. "I think it's out of anger how I got involved in voter's rights," said Mrs. White. Later she testified in an important civil rights case, *United States of America v. C.C. Campbell, et al.*, about the discrimination she had experienced. Finally, during Freedom Summer in 1964, when civil rights workers and college students came to Mississippi to help African Americans, she and her husband, Dorsey White Jr., registered. In November they cast their ballots for the first time.

When Stacy voted for the first time, it was not a presidential election year. She voted on state and local issues, and made her decisions by talking with her parents about things going on in their community, and reading her hometown newspaper in the college library. From then on she has voted in every election except one while she was away at college.

Then, in 2013, when the Supreme Court struck down a critical part of the Voting Rights Act of 1965, Stacy was outraged. "The VRA allowed me to vote as an African American," she said. "The 2013 Supreme Court decision is the most egregious decision ever made. It was an injustice!"

Civil rights leaders and concerned citizens everywhere were furious. "The Supreme Court stuck a dagger into the heart of the Voting Rights Act," said Congressman John Lewis of Georgia, who helped organize and lead the march from Selma to Montgomery in 1965 when he was chairman of SNCC.

The VRA had been passed in 1965 to protect minority voters. In 1970, Congress renewed it for five years in areas with histories of discriminatory practices, and reauthorized it several more times. Section 5 provided that voting procedures and election laws could not be changed without federal approval. Section 4 named the states, and districts within those states—such as Selma, Alabama—where the right to vote had been denied because of racial discrimination. Shelby County had a history of voting violations. But the county filed suit against the attorney general, Eric Holder Jr., and claimed that sections 4 and 5 were unconstitutional. The case, *Shelby County v. Holder*, came before the Supreme Court.

Justice Antonin Scalia maintained that the VRA was based on forty-year-old facts and was no longer relevant. Justice Sonia Sotomayor challenged his opinion and said, "Do you think racial discrimination has ended?" Nevertheless, the court voted in favor of declaring sections 4 and 5 of the VRA unconstitutional. The majority decided that no one was particularly racist these days. "Things had changed dramatically" in the South during the past fifty years. Justice Ruth Bader Ginsburg sharply disagreed, and blasted her colleagues. She denounced their decision as a brazen act of arrogance. Justice Ginsburg quoted an FBI investigation of Alabama legislators who referred to black voters as "Aborigines" and talked about how to keep them from the polls. "These conversations occurred not in the 1870s, or even in the 1960s," she said, "they took place in 2010." The VRA was a landmark law, she wrote, a solution to an important problem in American history.

Overwhelming evidence showed that states were still attempting to prevent people from voting with new discriminatory laws. People began to call this voter suppression. On the very day of the *Shelby County v. Holder* ruling, Texas enacted one of the strictest photo ID laws in the country. Registered voters were required to present photo IDs at the polls. But thousands of poor African Americans and Latinos, as well as elderly people, did not have cars, so they had no driver's

Ruth Bader Ginsburg on August 10, 1993, the day she was sworn in as a Supreme Court Justice.

licenses with their pictures, or the money to pay for photo IDs. So they were stopped from voting. Some seniors couldn't find their IDs and therefore couldn't vote.

In Alabama, more than thirty percent of voting-age citizens lived too far away from the nearest state office to obtain IDs. And the offices were open only two days a week, adding another obstacle.

Segregationists cooked up other ruses. They closed polls early to prevent working-class black and Hispanic voters from arriving in time to cast their ballots. Black people were kept longer at work on Election Day to make sure they didn't vote. And polling places were purposely located in dangerous neighborhoods to discourage black and Hispanic voters from going there. A bill was passed in North Carolina eliminating same-day registration and ending a preregistration program for sixteen- and seventeen-year-olds. These harmful election law changes would have been prevented by Section 5 of the VRA.

Commentators and bloggers protested.

"Congress Must Keep Its Voting Rights Act Promise."

"To Protect Democracy, Supreme Court Must Fully Uphold Voting Rights Act."

"Let America vote," wrote actor Bradley Whitford on behalf of Let America Vote, a campaign demanding that Congress reinstate the heart of the VRA.

A bipartisan (Republican and Democratic) group of lawmakers introduced multiple bills to strengthen the VRA and restore the protection it once provided. In 2015 Congressman John Lewis introduced a Voting Rights Advancement Act that would give the attorney general power to place federal observers at the polls. Because Lewis had been attacked on Bloody Sunday in 1965 marching for the right to vote, the issue had particular urgency for him.

Marcia McMillan Edwards was eleven years old when she marched right behind Lewis. She was trampled to the ground by other marchers trying to get away from the troopers' billy clubs. Years later she said: "The right to vote was attained by the suffering and ultimate sacrifices of many dedicated civil rights activists and foot soldiers. It is the duty of every eligible person in the United States to vote. Too many have fought and died for everyone to have the right to vote."

At the 2018 midterm election, artist Amy Huntington illustrated her message: "Shout VOTE! If young people vote everything WILL change."

Reginald E. Moore marched from Selma to Montgomery just before his eleventh birthday with a few neighborhood friends. His mother told them to stay together. "I was the youngest in the group," recalled Moore. When he arrived home, he found out that his mother had been beaten on the Edmund Pettus Bridge and had been taken to the hospital, where she died. "Two days later I turned eleven," said Moore, "and my life as a child would never be the same. My mother was very active in the movement, and through her I began to see and realize the importance of the struggle."

CHAPTER 16: VOTING FROM THE GRAVE

"I feel I'm not wanted in this state."

—Anthony Settles, a retiree in Texas

"REPUBLICANS ARE SYSTEMATICALLY AND DELIBERATELY trying to stop millions of American citizens from voting," said Hillary Clinton in 2015. She referred to laws backed by Republicans and passed in states across the country requiring that voters present an ID when they show up at the polling place.

"The intent of this law is to suppress the vote," said Anthony Settles, a retiree in Texas. Settles had been repeatedly blocked from voting because his mother had changed his last name when he was a teenager. Now, fifty years later, he couldn't find the paperwork documenting the change. He spent months looking for it and finally gave up. "I feel I'm not wanted in this state," said Settles.

Republicans worried as the voting-age population became less white and more African American, Latino, and Asian. Polls showed that these groups would be more

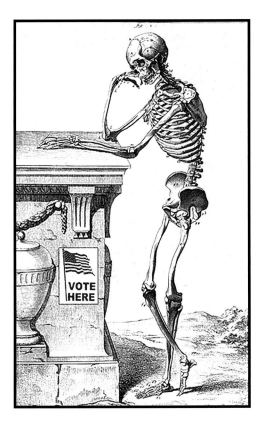

To humorously illustrate an article declaring that presidential elections are too long, Lorraine Devon Wilke added a "Vote Here" sticker to an image of a skeleton leaning on a plinth as it decides how to cast its ballot.

likely to vote Democratic. Republicans didn't want people who were not going to vote for them to vote at all. Studies show that they barred people of color from the ballot box with their new laws. A great percentage of black, Native American, and Latino voters couldn't vote in the 2016 election because they were told that they lacked the proper identification such as a driver's license or credit card. Or they were incorrectly informed that they weren't listed on voter rolls. And they had trouble finding polling sites because the locations had purposely been changed at the last minute. The Public Religion Research Institute documented this when it conducted a poll in 2018 asking Americans about their voting experiences. The survey showed that voter suppression was widespread, creating an advantage for Republicans.

"I don't want everybody to vote," admitted Paul Weyrich, a founder of the Heritage Foundation and the American Legislative Exchange Council, which helped write legislation to suppress voting. Republicans maintain that a lower turnout yields a more informed electorate.

The new laws alarmed civil rights leaders. They were reminded of the days when African Americans in the South were unfairly required to take a literacy test, or know the number of feathers on a chicken, in order to register to vote. As if rolling back to those times, the Supreme Court decision in 2013 had sharply reduced parts of the Voting Rights Act that protected African Americans and others, especially in states with a history of discrimination.

As the November 2018 midterm election approached, four veteran volunteers of Freedom Summer returned to Mississippi for a voter registration campaign. The volunteers, now in their seventies, joined a nonpartisan youth group, Mississippi Votes, to help register hundreds of thousands of voters.

Howard Kirschenbaum, a veteran volunteer, said that memories came flooding back as he watched students waiting to fill out registration forms at the University of Mississippi. "They want to vote," he said. "They are able to vote. This is what we worked for all those years ago."

When accused of voter suppression, Republicans retaliate by charging Democrats with voter fraud. In the 2000 St. Louis, Missouri, election, they claimed that Democrats were using the names of dead people—the cemetery vote. Sen. Christopher "Kit" Bond of Missouri found one alderman, an elected official, who had died but whose name was still on the voter registrations rolls.

Artist Barry Blitt illustrated an article protesting voter ID cards, and pointed out the absurdity of charges of voter fraud by portraying fantasy characters and a dog casting their ballots at the poll.

However, the senator couldn't prove that anyone had used the alderman's name in order to vote. At the end of the investigation in Missouri, it was clear that out of 2.3 million voters, only four people had committed some kind of fraud.

The cemetery vote, also known as ghost voting, was nothing new. Back in 1860, when Abraham Lincoln was the Republican candidate for president, he ran against Democrat John Breckinridge of Kentucky. To ensure Breckinridge's win in the North as well as in the South, Tammany Hall gangs registered nearly a thousand false names, including those of hundreds of dead people.

More recently in Kansas, Republican Kris Kobach was running for secretary of state in 2010. Kobach declared that he had found evidence that two thousand dead voters were still registered to vote. For example, Kobach accused Albert K. Brewer of Wichita of voting from the grave. But Brewer, age seventy-eight, was very much alive, and was stunned to hear the news of his death as he did chores in his front yard. "I don't think this is heaven, not when I'm raking leaves," said Brewer.

Nevertheless, Kobach was elected Kansas's secretary of state, and under his command a law was passed in 2011 requiring people to prove their citizenship before registering to vote. But in 2018 a federal judge struck down the law as unconstitutional.

Undaunted, Kobach spread stories alleging that out-of-state students voted twice, and that noncitizens cast ballots. He stated that illegal immigration and voter fraud were destroying the nation. President Donald Trump approved of

Kobach's efforts and appointed him vice chairman of a voter fraud commission dedicated to rooting out illegal voters. However, the commission was dissolved in January 2018 because the members couldn't find any proof of widespread fraud.

Yet voter fraud is easy to accomplish, wrote journalist John Fund. Fund reported that New York City's Department of Investigation sent undercover agents to sixty-three Manhattan polling places in the fall of 2014. The agents pretended to be registered voters. They assumed the names of people who were dead, had moved out of town, or were sitting in jail. One young female agent gave the name of a woman who

When Missouri senator Kit Bond fumed that dogs and dead people were voting, Barry Blitt drew a picture of a little dog showing its ID to a registrar.

had died in 2012 at the age of eighty-seven. The workers at the polling site gave the agent a ballot, no questions asked. Ninety-seven percent of the time the agents were allowed to vote. But to keep the election results fair, they simply wrote in votes for a candidate they named "John Test."

The most absurd case of alleged voter fraud occurred in the 2000 St. Louis, Missouri, election. In a relentless campaign to clean up the voting system, Republican senator Bond blamed Democrats for using the names of dogs to vote. In fact, a prankster had registered a thirteen-year-old springer spaniel named Ritzy Meckler to vote. Yet there was no record of Ritzy casting a ballot. Election Board workers finally discovered her identity. Ritzy became Senator Bond's mascot as he pushed for mandating photo IDs at the polls. He posed for pictures with Ritzy and said that he liked dogs, but added, "I do not think we should allow them to vote."

CHAPTER 17: THE GERRY-MANDER AND OTHER MONSTERS

"I've always voted. But now I feel that my vote doesn't count."

—Emily Bunting, resident of Richland County, Wisconsin

ON MARCH 26, 1812, THE *BOSTON GAZETTE* PUBLISHED A POLITICAL cartoon of a map showing Republican districts wound around Boston to avoid pockets of Federalist support. The shape of the districts resembled a "horrid monster" with claws, wings, and a dragon-like head. When the editor of the *Gazette* posted the cartoon on his office wall he noticed that the districts looked like a salamander. "Call it a Gerrymander," he said.

The name referred to Elbridge Gerry, a Founding Father who was a delegate at the Constitutional Convention. In 1810, Gerry was elected governor of Massachusetts. During his second term of office, Gerry signed into law a redistricting plan designed to give his Republican party an advantage. Artist Elkanah Tisdale pointed out the grotesque truth about redistricting in his cartoon version of the map, labeled "The Gerry-Mander."

The name stuck, and so did the monstrous practice. Although the Federalists won more votes in 1812, the Republicans won more seats in the Senate. Gerry lost his bid for reelection as governor, but he is remembered as the namesake of gerrymandering, a partisan process for stealing an election.

The monster is still out there. In 2011, for instance, the Republican-controlled legislature of Wisconsin secretly redrew the boundaries of voting districts. The new map helped their party but harmed Democratic voters, who were "packed" into a few districts where they usually won a majority of votes anyway. Emily Bunting's district in Richland County was "cracked," placing her family in a

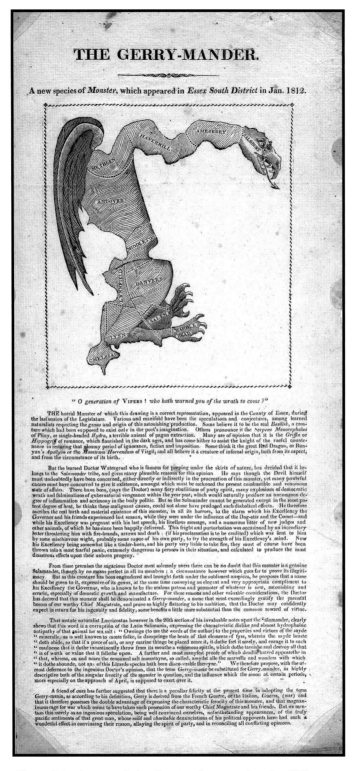

The original page of the *Boston Gazette* showing "The Gerry-Mander. A new species of Monster," January 1812.

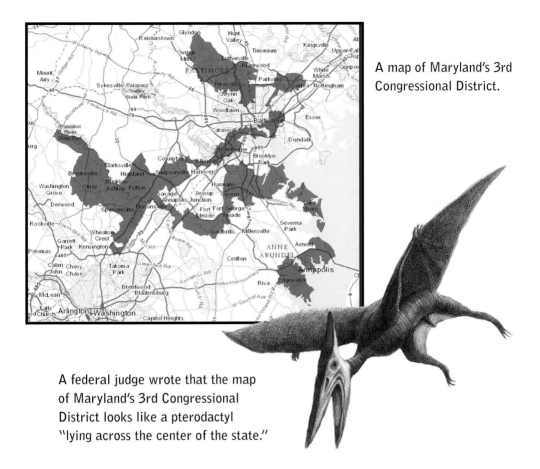

A map of Maryland's 3rd Congressional District.

A federal judge wrote that the map of Maryland's 3rd Congressional District looks like a pterodactyl "lying across the center of the state."

different community with a new representative. When she called her Republican representative about problems such as poor roads, she was ignored.

Wendy Sue Johnson in Eau Claire also found herself in a new district, although she had not moved. Suddenly many of her neighbors right across the street voted in a different district. The boundary ran alongside Johnson's house.

William Whitford, a former law professor from Madison, met with Johnson, Bunting, and nine other Wisconsin Democrats. They claimed that the redistricting was unconstitutional, and they filed a lawsuit to get rid of the map. The case went all the way to the Supreme Court. But the plaintiffs (Whitford and the eleven others) lost because they failed to show how they were harmed personally by the old trick of gerrymandering.

Republicans aren't the only ones guilty of rigging an election with a gerrymandered map. In 2000, Democrats redrew Maryland's 3rd Congressional District to favor their party. The bizarre shape looked like a "broken-winged pterodactyl, lying prostrate across the center of the state," observed a federal judge. Some people said the crazily drawn Third District resembled a praying mantis. The district is one of the most gerrymandered in the country.

Another is Illinois's Fourth District in Chicago. Democrats packed two Latino parts of Chicago into a single district. They linked the Puerto Rican North Side community to the Mexican American South Side by a slender strip of highway. The resulting shape is known as "the earmuffs." Voters in the mostly Latino district benefit from the earmuffs. Rather than being tuned out, they can make their voices heard on issues such as immigration due to their large numbers.

As Matt Lewis wrote in the Daily Beast, "Democrats hate gerrymandering—except when they get to do it."

Many people hoped that the Supreme Court would declare gerrymandering illegal. However, in 2019 the Court declared that Federal Courts could not resolve the question of partisan gerrymandering. Elected branches of government, they declared, must deal with the issue.

CHAPTER 18: WE WANT CHANGE!

"We may be young but our voices are louder than you can imagine."

—Sarah Chadwick, student at Marjory Stoneman Douglas High School

ON VALENTINE'S DAY 2018, A GUNMAN KILLED SEVENTEEN students at Marjory Stoneman Douglas High School in Parkland, Florida. Days after the massacre, Parkland students leaped into action and demanded stricter gun laws in the United States. A month later, on March 14, they organized a National School Walkout to protest the epidemic of school shootings. On that day, at 10:00 a.m., the time of the shooting, nearly a million students across the country walked out of their classrooms for seventeen minutes, one minute for each of the victims. Like the kids in Selma, Alabama, in 1963, they took matters into their own hands and risked being suspended from school, or even expelled, to stand up for their beliefs.

"By more than one school doing this," said Audrey Diaz, a senior at Marjory Stoneman Douglas High School in 2018, "it shows politicians and lawmakers that we want change to happen."

At Case Elementary School in Akron, Ohio, fifth-graders joined the nationwide protest. They were inspired by a class assignment to write about the Birmingham Children's Crusade in 1963, when more than a thousand students skipped school to march for civil rights. The ten- and eleven-year-olds in Ohio drew posters honoring the students killed in Parkland, and they marched out of their classrooms at the appointed time. "Adults have been protesting against things," said fifth-grader Maeva Lile, "but nothing has changed that much." And no new legislation has been passed.

Most of the students who participated in the National School Walkout

Students from Marjory Stoneman Douglas High School stand together on stage with other young victims of gun violence at the conclusion of the March for Our Lives rally on March 24, 2018.

were not yet of voting age, and therefore unable to elect lawmakers whose decisions affect their lives. "High schoolers lack any real power," wrote Laurence Steinberg in the *New York Times*. "This needs to change: The federal voting age in the United States should be lowered from 18 to 16."

In Chicago a group of students calling themselves ChicagoStrong organized another protest against gun violence. At 10:00 a.m. on Saturday, July 7, 2018, thousands of people marched onto the northbound lanes of traffic on the Dan Ryan Expressway and shut it down for hours. On the overpasses above the highway, more demonstrators waved signs that read STOP THIS SENSELESS VIOLENCE.

"Too many people are shot and killed in our city each week," stated the group on its website, "but our stories never gain national attention. We need America to hear our voices too because Chicago's problems are America's problems."

Rev. Jesse Jackson, a leader of the demonstration, said they were peacefully marching to point out the need for education, jobs, and justice on the city's South Side and West Side, heavily populated by African Americans.

Many people agree that high schoolers care about local and national problems and should be allowed to vote. Studies prove that teenagers can gather and process information, weighing pros and cons as well as most adults. Research conducted by FairVote shows that sixteen- and seventeen-year-olds are as informed and engaged in political issues as older voters. If they start voting in their teens, they are more likely to make voting a lifelong habit and increase voter turnout.

In November 2013, Takoma Park, Maryland, a suburb of Washington, D.C., granted sixteen- and seventeen-year-olds the right to vote in local elections. Other cities such as Hyattsville, Maryland, and Berkeley, California, followed and have lowered the voting age. Many of these kids hold jobs to help their families and are paying taxes. So communities believe that they should have the right to make their voices heard at the ballot box.

In California in 2017, a law was launched allowing sixteen- and seventeen-year-olds to preregister online, or at the Department of Motor Vehicles when they applied for driver's licenses. Then they would automatically be eligible to vote when they turned eighteen. A group called Inspire U.S. has been registering high school students in their classrooms.

The kids who marched in Selma, Alabama, back in the 1960s knew exactly how important the vote was for their parents, and would be for them when they were able to vote. "Thirteen- to eighteen-year-olds took to the streets against the counsel of parents, elders, and teachers," recalled Colia Lafayette, a leader who recruited students at Hudson High School. "While you can't vote yet," she told them, "you can teach and educate your parents to vote. Voting is power!"

In spring 2018 country singer and activist Willie Nelson talked to young people who were protesting guns after the Florida shootings. Nelson said to the kids, "If you see something you don't like out there, you vote 'em out." Inspired, he wrote a new song, "Vote 'Em Out!"

Nelson was particularly focusing on young people who would be voting for the first time in November 2018 and "are very excited about it." He said, "If you like who's in there, leave 'em in." And he sang:

If you don't like who's in there, vote 'em out.

That's what Election Day is all about.

Maybe these young people can change things when they finally get the vote.

Bobby Simmons wearing zinc oxide on his forehead printed with the word "VOTE" as he marched from Selma to Montgomery, Alabama, March 1965.

TIMELINE OF VOTING RIGHTS IN THE UNITED STATES

1776—The Declaration of Independence is signed. Voting is restricted to men who own land and are at least twenty-one years old. Voting laws are set by each individual state legislature instead of the federal government.

1787—Delegates to the Constitutional Convention adopt the U.S. Constitution. States retain the right to regulate their own voting laws. Landowning men who are citizens and twenty-one or older are still the only people allowed to vote.

1790—The 1790 Naturalization Law is passed, allowing only "free white" immigrants to become naturalized citizens.

1848—Women's rights convention is held in Seneca Falls, New York.

1848—The Treaty of Guadalupe Hidalgo ends the Mexican-American War and grants U.S. citizenship to Mexicans living in newly gained territories. However, English language requirements and intimidation prevent many new citizens from voting.

1865—North Carolina becomes the last state to remove a property-ownership requirement for voting.

1866—The Civil Rights Act of 1866 grants citizenship to native-born Americans. However, it does not grant all citizens the right to vote.

1868—The Fourteenth Amendment is ratified, granting citizenship to former slaves.

1870—The Fifteenth Amendment is ratified, making it illegal to deny anyone the right to vote based on race. However, individual states enact measures aimed at preventing African American citizens and others from voting.

1876—The Supreme Court rules in *Elk v. Wilkins* that Native Americans are not citizens as defined by the Fourteenth Amendment.

1882—The Chinese Exclusion Act is passed by Congress, barring people of Chinese ancestry from becoming U.S. citizens.

1887—The Dawes Act is passed, granting citizenship to Native Americans who agree to give up tribal affiliations.

1890—Wyoming is admitted to the U.S. and becomes the first state to allow women to vote in state and local elections. However, women cannot vote in federal elections.

1890—The Indian Naturalization Act is passed, allowing Native Americans to apply for citizenship. These applications are processed as if indigenous people were immigrants.

1919—Native Americans who served in the military during World War I are granted citizenship.

1920—The Nineteenth Amendment is passed, giving women the right to vote in all state and federal elections.

1922—The Supreme Court rules in *Ozawa v. United States* that people of Japanese heritage cannot become citizens.

1923—The Supreme Court rules in *United States v. Bhagat Singh Thind* that people of Asian Indian and other Asian ancestries cannot become citizens.

1924—The Snyder Act (also called the Indian Citizen Act) is passed, giving citizenship to Native Americans, but many states enact laws that continue to suppress voting.

1943—The Magnuson Act is passed, repealing the Chinese Exclusion Act and allowing people of Chinese ancestry to become citizens.

1952—The McCarran-Walter Act is passed, allowing people of Asian ancestry to become citizens.

1961—The Twenty-Third Amendment allows citizens of Washington, D.C., to vote for the U.S. president for the first time. However, District of Columbia residents remain without voting representation in Congress.

1962— New Mexico becomes the last state to grant Native Americans the vote.

1963—Martin Luther King delivers his "I Have a Dream" speech to more than two hundred fifty thousand people participating in the March on Washington.

1964—The Twenty-Fourth Amendment is passed, abolishing poll taxes.

1964—The Mississippi Freedom Summer Project, a voter registration drive organized by a coalition of civil rights organizations, takes place.

1965—A voting rights campaign in Selma, Alabama, culminates in the fifty-four-mile Alabama Freedom March to the state capitol in Montgomery.

1965—The Voting Rights Act is passed, forbidding states from imposing discriminatory restrictions on voting.

1971—The Twenty-Sixth Amendment is passed, lowering the voting age to eighteen.

1975—Amendments to the Voting Rights Act require that ballots and voting instructions be printed in languages besides English.

1993—The National Voter Registration Act (also called the Motor Voter Act) is passed, making it easier to register to vote by making registration available at motor vehicle departments and other agencies.

AMENDMENTS TO THE U.S. CONSTITUTION DISCUSSED IN THIS BOOK

AMENDMENT XII

Passed by Congress December 9, 1803. Ratified June 15, 1804.

AMENDMENT XIII

Passed by Congress January 31, 1865. Ratified December 6, 1865.

Note: A portion of Article IV, section 2, of the Constitution was superseded by the Thirteenth Amendment.

Section 1.

Neither slavery nor involuntary servitude, except as a punishment for crime whereof the party shall have been duly convicted, shall exist within the United States, or any place subject to their jurisdiction.

Section 2.

Congress shall have power to enforce this article by appropriate legislation.

AMENDMENT XIV

Passed by Congress June 13, 1866. Ratified July 9, 1868.

Note: Article I, section 2, of the Constitution was modified by section 2 of the Fourteenth Amendment.

Section 1.

All persons born or naturalized in the United States, and subject to the jurisdiction thereof, are citizens of the United States and of the State wherein they reside. No State shall make or enforce any law which shall abridge the privileges or immunities of citizens of the United States; nor shall any State deprive any person of life, liberty, or property, without due process of law; nor deny to any person within its jurisdiction the equal protection of the laws.

Section 2.

Representatives shall be apportioned among the several States according to their respective numbers, counting the whole number of persons in each State, excluding Indians not taxed. But when the right to vote at any election for the choice of electors for President and Vice-President of the United States, Representatives in Congress, the Executive and Judicial officers of a State, or the members of the Legislature thereof, is denied to any of the male inhabitants of such State, being twenty-one years of age,* and citizens of the United States, or in any way abridged, except for participation in rebellion, or other crime, the basis of representation therein shall be reduced in the proportion which the number of such male citizens shall bear to the whole number of male citizens twenty-one years of age in such State. **

Section 3.

No person shall be a Senator or Representative in Congress, or elector of President and Vice-President, or hold any office, civil or military, under the United States, or under any State, who, having previously taken an oath, as a member of Congress, or as an officer of the United States, or as a member of any State legislature, or as an executive or judicial officer of any State, to support the Constitution of the United States, shall have engaged in insurrection or rebellion against the same, or given aid or comfort to the enemies thereof. But Congress may by a vote of two-thirds of each House, remove such disability.

Section 4.

The validity of the public debt of the United States, authorized by law, including debts incurred for payment of pensions and bounties for services in suppressing insurrection or rebellion, shall not be questioned. But neither the United States nor any State shall assume or pay any debt or obligation incurred in aid of insurrection or rebellion against the United States, or any claim for the loss or emancipation of any slave; but all such debts, obligations and claims shall be held illegal and void.

Section 5.

The Congress shall have the power to enforce, by appropriate legislation, the provisions of this article.

* *Changed by section 1 of the Twenty-Sixth Amendment.*

** A portion of Article II, section 1 of the Constitution was superseded by the 12th amendment. The Electors shall meet in their respective states and vote by ballot for President and Vice-President, one of whom, at least, shall not be an inhabitant of the same state with themselves; they shall name in their ballots the person voted for as President, and in distinct ballots the person voted for as Vice-President, and they shall make distinct lists of all persons voted for as President, and of all persons voted for as Vice-President, and of the number of votes for each, which lists they shall sign and certify, and transmit sealed to the seat of the government of the United States, directed to the President of the Senate; — the President of the Senate shall, in the presence of the Senate and House of Representatives, open all the certificates and the votes shall then be counted; — The person having the greatest number of votes for President, shall be the President, if such number be a majority of the whole number of Electors appointed; and if no person have such majority, then from the persons having the highest numbers not exceeding three on the list of those voted for as President, the House of Representatives shall choose immediately, by ballot, the President. But in choosing the President, the votes shall be taken by states, the representation from each state having one vote; a quorum for this purpose shall consist of a member or members from two-thirds of the states, and a majority of all the states shall be necessary to a choice. [And if the House of Representatives shall not choose a President whenever the right of choice shall devolve upon them, before the fourth day of March next following, then the Vice-President shall act as President, as in case of the death or other constitutional disability of the President. —]* The person having the greatest number of votes as Vice-President, shall be the Vice-President, if such number be a majority of the whole number of Electors appointed, and if no person have a majority, then from the two highest numbers on the list, the Senate shall choose the Vice-President; a quorum for the purpose shall consist of two-thirds of the whole number of Senators, and a majority of the whole number shall be necessary to a choice. But no person constitutionally ineligible to the office of President shall be eligible to that of Vice-President of the United States. *Superseded by section 3 of the 20th amendment.

AMENDMENT XV
Passed by Congress February 26, 1869. Ratified February 3, 1870.

Section 1.

The right of citizens of the United States to vote shall not be denied or abridged by the United States or by any State on account of race, color, or previous condition of servitude--

Section 2.

The Congress shall have the power to enforce this article by appropriate legislation.

AMENDMENT XIX
Passed by Congress June 4, 1919. Ratified August 18, 1920.

The right of citizens of the United States to vote shall not be denied or abridged by the United States or by any State on account of sex.

Congress shall have power to enforce this article by appropriate legislation.

AMENDMENT XXII
Passed by Congress March 21, 1947. Ratified February 27, 1951.

Section 1.

No person shall be elected to the office of the President more than twice, and no person who has held the office of President, or acted as President, for more than two years of a term to which some other person was elected President shall be elected to the office of the President more than once. But this Article shall not apply to any person holding the office of President when this Article was proposed by the Congress, and shall not prevent any person who may be holding the office of President, or acting as President, during the term within which this Article becomes operative from holding the office of President or acting as President during the remainder of such term.

Section 2.

This article shall be inoperative unless it shall have been ratified as an amendment to the Constitution by the legislatures of three-fourths of the several States within seven years from the date of its submission to the States by the Congress.

AMENDMENT XXIV

Passed by Congress August 27, 1962. Ratified January 23, 1964.

Section 1.

The right of citizens of the United States to vote in any primary or other election for President or Vice President, for electors for President or Vice President, or for Senator or Representative in Congress, shall not be denied or abridged by the United States or any State by reason of failure to pay any poll tax or other tax.

Section 2.

The Congress shall have power to enforce this article by appropriate legislation.

AMENDMENT XXVI

Passed by Congress March 23, 1971. Ratified July 1, 1971.

Note: Amendment 14, section 2, of the Constitution was modified by section 1 of the Twenty-Sixth Amendment.

Section 1.

The right of citizens of the United States, who are eighteen years of age or older, to vote shall not be denied or abridged by the United States or by any State on account of age.

Section 2.

The Congress shall have power to enforce this article by appropriate legislation.

SOURCES

BOOKS

Anderson, Carol, with Tonya Bolden. *We Are Not Yet Equal: Understanding Our Racial Divide.* New York: Bloomsbury, 2018.

Bausum, Ann. *With Courage and Cloth: Winning the Fight for a Woman's Right to Vote.* Washington, D.C. : National Geographic Society, 2004.

Berman, Ari. *Give Us the Ballot: The Modern Struggle for Voting Rights in America.* New York: Picador, 2015.

Bordewich, Fergus M. *The First Congress: How James Madison, George Washington, and a Group of Extraordinary Men Invented the Government.* New York: Simon & Schuster, 2016.

Campbell, Tracy. *Deliver the Vote: A History of Election Fraud, an American Political Tradition—1742–2004.* New York: Carroll & Graf, 2005.

Carter, Rosalynn. *First Lady from Plains.* Boston: Houghton Mifflin, 1984.

Chernow, Ron. *Alexander Hamilton.* New York: Penguin Books, 2004.

Conkling, Winifred. *Votes for Women!: American Suffragists and the Battle for the Ballot.* Chapel Hill, NC: Algonquin, 2018.

Daley, David. *Rat F**ked: Why Your Vote Doesn't Count.* New York: Liveright, 2017.

Dittmer, John. *Local People: The Struggle for Civil Rights in Mississippi.* Urbana: University of Illinois Press, 1994.

DuBois, Ellen Carol. *Feminism & Suffrage.* Ithaca, NY: Cornell University Press, 1978.

Freedman, Russell. *Angel Island.* New York: Clarion Books, 2013.

———. *Vietnam: A History of the War.* New York: Holiday House, 2016.

Gitin, Maria. *This Bright Light of Ours: Stories from the Voting Rights Fight.* Tuscaloosa: University of Alabama Press, 2014.

Greve, Michael S. *The Constitution: Understanding America's Founding Document.* Washington, D.C.: AEI, 2013.

Hamer, Fannie Lou, Maegan Parker Brooks, and Davis W. Houck, eds. *The Speeches of Fannie Lou Hamer: To Tell It Like It Is.* Jackson, Mississippi: University Press of Mississippi, 2011.

Hernandez, Daniel, with Susan Goldman Rubin. *They Call Me a Hero: A Memoir of My Youth.* New York: Simon & Schuster, 2013.

Holton, Woody. *Abigail Adams.* New York: Free Press, 2009.

Keyssar, Alexander. *The Right to Vote: The Contested History of Democracy in the United States.* New York: Basic Books, 2000.

Klarman, Michael J. *The Framers' Coup: The Making of the United States Constitution.* New York: Oxford University Press, 2016.

Levinson, Cynthia. *We've Got a Job: The 1963 Birmingham Children's March.* Atlanta: Peachtree, 2012.

Lowery, Lynda Blackmon, as told to Elspeth Leacock and Susan Buckley. *Turning 15 on the Road to Freedom.* New York: Penguin, 2015.

May, Gary. *Bending Toward Justice: The Voting Rights Act and the Transformation of American Democracy.* New York: Basic Books, 2013.

McCarter, Jeremy. *Young Radicals: In the War for American Ideals.* New York: Random House, 2017.

McKissack, Patricia, and Fredrick McKissack. *Mary Church Terrell: Leader for Equality*. Berkeley Heights, NJ: Enslow, 1991.

Mills, Kay. *This Little Light of Mine: The Life of Fannie Lou Hamer*. Lexington: University Press of Kentucky, 2007.

Minnite, Lorraine C. *The Myth of Voter Fraud*. Ithaca, NY: Cornell University Press, 2010.

O'Brien, Mary Barmeyer. *Jeannette Rankin: Bright Star in the Big Sky*. Guilford, CT: Rowman & Littlefield, 2015.

Partridge, Elizabeth. *Marching for Freedom*. New York: Viking, 2009.

Rubin, Susan Goldman. *Freedom Summer: The 1964 Struggle for Civil Rights in Mississippi*. New York: Holiday House, 2014.

Stevens, Doris. *Jailed for Freedom: American Women Win the Right to Vote*. Edited by Carol O'Hare. Troutdale, OR: New Sage Press, 1995.

Stewart, David O. *The Summer of 1787*. New York: Simon & Schuster, 2007.

Terrell, Mary Church. *A Colored Woman in a White World*. Amherst, NY: Humanity Books, 2005.

Webb, Sheyann, and Rachel West Nelson. *Selma, Lord, Selma*. Tuscaloosa: University of Alabama Press, 1997.

Woelfle, Gretchen. *Jeanette Rankin: Political Pioneer*. Honesdale, PA: Calkins Creek, 2007.

NEWSPAPERS AND MAGAZINES

Anderson, Carol. "The Voter Fraud Lie." *New York Times*, September 9, 2018.

Azure, Jamie. "North Dakota's Voter-ID Law Aimed to Silence Native American Voters." *Washington Post*, November 1, 2018.

Baltimore Sun. Editorial, March 8, 2018.

Berman, Ari. "Welcome to the First Presidential Election Since Voting Rights Act Gutted." *Rolling Stone*, June 23, 2016.

Blight, David W. "Our Debt to Frederick Douglass." *New York Times*, November 6, 2018.

Boston Gazette. "The Gerry-Mander. A New species of *Monster*, which appeared in Essex South District in Jan. 1812." March 26, 1812.

Burch, Audra D. S. "Voter Registration Drive Gets Reinforcements." *New York Times*, September 26, 2018.

Decker, Cathleen. "Why Young Voters Are Flocking to Sanders and Older Ones to Clinton." *Los Angeles Times*, April 19, 2016.

Foderaro, Lisa W. "Fresh-Faced and Fervent, the Young Get Political." *New York Times*, September 29, 2017.

Gearan, Anne, and Niraj Chokshi. "Hillary Clinton Calls for Sweeping Expansion of Voter Access." *Washington Post*, June 4, 2015.

Gitlin, Todd. "Voting and Racism." Letter to the editor, *New York Times*, October 25, 2017.

Goldstein, Dana. "Along with Class Photos, Political Views Find a Place in High School Yearbooks." *New York Times*, May 22, 2017.

Gupta, Vania. "The Voter Purges Are Coming." *New York Times*, July 19, 2017.

Horwitz, Sari. "Getting a Photo ID So You Can Vote Is Easy. Unless You're Poor, Black, Latino or Elderly." *Washington Post*, May 23, 2016.

Klaas, Brian. "Gerrymandering Is the Biggest Obstacle to Genuine Democracy in the United States. So Why Is No One Protesting?" *Washington Post*, February 10, 2017.

Lepore, Jill. "Rock, Paper, Scissors: How We Used to Vote." *New Yorker*, October 13, 2008.

Lewis, Randy. "Willie Nelson's Musical Message to Fans Ahead of Midterms: 'Vote 'Em Out.'" *Los Angeles Times*, October 26, 2018.

Liptak, Adam. "New on Law School Syllabus This Fall: Trump's Actions." *New York Times*, August 15, 2017.

Morris, G. Elliott. "How Much Can the Youth Vote Actually Help the Democrats?" *New York Times*, September 15, 2017.

New York Times. "The Bogus Voter-Fraud Commission." Editorial, July 23, 2017.

New York Times. "Trump Voters, One Year In." Editorial, January 18, 2018.

Osnos, Evan, David Remmick, and Joshua Yaffa. "Trump, Putin, and the New Cold War." *New Yorker*, March 6, 2017.

Pager, Tyler. "Obama Endorses New Graduate for Connecticut Senate." *New York Times*, October 9, 2018.

Peck, Jason. Letter to the editor, *New York Times*, January 17, 2018.

Plumer, Brad. "A Climate Report That Changes Minds? Don't Bet on It." *New York Times*, November 5, 2017.

Reilly, Katie. "A New North Dakota Law Threatened Native American Votes." *Time*, November 7, 2018.

Robertson, Emily. Letter to the editor, *New York Times*, January 17, 2018.

Rubin, Rebekkah. "A Banner Held High." *Oberlin Alumni Magazine*, Winter 2018–2019.

Saul, Stephanie, and Anemona Hartocollis. "Too Young to Protest? 10-Year-Olds Beg to Differ." *New York Times*, March 14, 2018.

Schwartz, John. "Between the Lines of the Voting Rights Act Opinion." *New York Times*, June 25, 2013.

Sorkin, Amy Davidson. "The Court Rejects the Voting Rights Act—and History." *New Yorker*, June 25, 2013.

Staples, Brent. "How the Suffrage Movement Betrayed Black Women." *New York Times*, July 28, 2018.

Steinberg, Laurence. "Why We Should Lower the Voting Age to 16." *New York Times*, March 2, 2018.

Strauss, Valerie. "Florida Students Chanting 'We Want Change' Walk out of Schools to Protest Gun Violence." *Washington Post*, February 20, 2018.

Suprun, Christopher. "Why Electors Should Reject Trump." *New York Times*, December 6, 2016.

Wang, Amy. "Anti-gun Protesters Take Over Chicago Highway." *Washington Post*, July 7, 2018.

Woolsey, James R., and Brian J. Fox. "To Protect Voting, Use Open-Source." *New York Times*, October 3, 2017.

Yoon-Hendricks, Alexandra. "Teenagers Fight Climate Change, from the Front." *New York Times*, July 22, 2018.

ONLINE SOURCES

Austin-Hillery, Nicole. "Congress Must Keep Its voting Rights Promise." Billmoyers.com. August 6, 2014.

Benen, Steve. "Dems Renew Push for Voting Rights Act." *MaddowBlog*, June 24, 2015. http://www.msnbc.com/rachel-maddow-show/dems-renew-push-voting-rights-act.

Brennan Center for Justice. "The Voting Rights Act" (resource page). https://www.brennancenter.org/analysis/voting-rights-act-resource-page.

Dolasia, Meera. "American Students Stage a National Walkout to Plea for Stricter Gun Laws." DOGOnews, March 15, 2018. https://www.dogonews.com/2018/3/15/american-students-stage-a-national-walkout-to-plea-for-stricter-gun-laws.

East Tennessee Historical Society. "'Don't Forget to Be a Good Boy': Harry T. Burn's Letter from Mom and the Ratification of the 19th Amendment in Tennessee." http://www.teachtnhistory.org/File/Harry_T._Burn.pdf.

Fund, John. "Voter Fraud: We've Got Proof It's Easy." *National Review*, January 12, 2014. https://www.nationalreview.com/2014/01/voter-fraud-weve-got-proof-its-easy-john-fund/.

Grinberg, Emanuella, and Holly Yan. "A Generation Raised on Gun Violence Sends a Loud Message to Adults: Enough." CNN, updated March 16, 2018. https://www.cnn.com/2018/03/14/us/national-school-walkout-gun-violence-protests/index.html.

Haskall, Will. "Quote of the Day" Democratic Legislative Campaign Committee. dlcc.org/friday-five/friday-five-october-12-2018.

Hersh, Eitan. "How Democrats Suppress the Vote." ABC News, Nov. 3, 2015. https://fivethirtyeight.com/features/how-democrats-suppress-the-vote/.

Koch, Kathy. "Election Reform: Are Antiquated Voting Machines the Problem?" CQ Resear-cher, Volume 11, Issue 38, November 2, 2001. http://library.cqpress.com/cqresearcher/document.php?id=cqresrre2001110200.

Koranda, Jeannine. "Dead Folks Voting? At Least One's Still Alive." *Wichita Eagle*, October 29, 2010, updated August 8, 2014. https://www.kansas.com/news/politics-government/election/article1046914.html.

Lewis, Matt. "Democrats Hate Gerrymandering—Except When They Get to Do It." Daily Beast, April 2, 2018. https://www.thedailybeast.com/democrats-hate-gerrymandering-except-when-they-get-to-do-it.

Lopez, Tomas. "'Shelby County': One Year Later." Brennan Center for Justice, June 24, 2014. https://www.brennancenter.org/analysis/shelby-county-one-year-later.

Mikulich, Alex. "The Real Fraud in 'Voter Fraud.'" *JustSouth E-newsletter*, Number 21, August 2012. http://loyno.edu/jsri/real-fraud-"voter-fraud".

NoiseCat, Julian Brave. "Republicans Wanted to Suppress the Native American Vote. It's Working." *Guardian* (U.S. edition), October 26, 2018. https://www.theguardian.com/us-news/2018/oct/26/the-real-reason-for-voter-id-laws-to-prevent-native-americans-from-voting.

Pérez Myrna and Lucy Zhou. "To protect democracy, Supreme Court must fully uphold Voting Rights Act." *The Christian Science Monitor*. February 27, 2013.

Rainey, Ryan. "Ruth Bader Ginsburg Blasts Colleagues for 'Hubris' in Eviscerating Voting Rights Act." *Huffington Post*, June 25, 2013. https://www.huffingtonpost.com/2013/06/25/ruth-bader-ginsburg-voting-rights_n_3498905.html.

Whitaker, Morgan. "Scalia: Renewing Voting Rights Act a 'Perpetuation of Racial Entitlement.'" MSNBC, *PoliticsNation with Al Sharpton*, updated October 2, 2013. http://www.msnbc.com/politicsnation/scalia-renewing-voting-rights-act.

Whitford, Bill. "'I've Always Voted. But Now I Feel That My Vote Doesn't Count': Partisan Gerrymandering Silences Voters." Campaign

Legal Center, June 15, 2018. https://campaignlegal.org/story/ive-always-voted-now-i-feel-my-vote-doesnt-count-partisan-gerrymandering-silences-voters.

Whitford, Bradley. Let America Vote. https://www.letamericavote.org/?s=bradley+whitford&submit=.

BOOKLETS

National Voting Rights Museum & Institute. *Bridges: Bridging Our Past, Our Present, and Our Future Possibilities.* Selma, AL: Imani Press, undated.

———. *Bridges: The Story of the Voting Rights Struggle in Selma & the Black Belt.* Edited by Connie Tucker. Selma, AL: Imani Press, 2015.

———. *Celebrating and Honoring the Legacy of Student Foot Soldiers.* Program, November 7, 2015.

———. *Children of the Movement.* Selma, AL: Imani Press, 2017.

———. *21st Annual Living Legends, Honoring Students of the Civil and Voting Rights Movement During the 1960s.* November 7, 2015.

Tucker, Connie, and Abina D. Billups, eds. *50th Commemorative Book, Selma.* Atlanta, GA: Bridge Crossing Jubilee, 2015.

INTERVIEWS BY PHONE WITH AUTHOR

Davis, Wes. September 24, 2018, and October 3, 2018.

Hernandez, Daniel Jr. October 27, 2017.

Kibbe, Margaret. November 3, 2017.

Kolpas, Jake. October 29, 2017, and November 2, 2017.

Rubin, Andrew. October 23, 2017.

Walker, Pearlie (National Voting Rights Museum & Institute). March 20, 2017.

White, Stacy. November 3, 2017.

SOURCE NOTES

p. iv. "The right . . . almost sacred." Mikulich, online article.

PROLOGUE

p. 1. "North Dakota's . . . American voters." Azure, *Washington Post* article.

p. 1. "We didn't . . . vouched for us." Azure, *Washington Post* article.

p. 1. "This is . . . an insult." NoiseCat, online article.

p. 2. DON'T DISENFRANCHISE . . . COULDN'T REMOVE. Reilly, *Time* article.

p. 2. "But then . . . make a statement." Reilly, *Time* article.

CHAPTER 1

p. 4. "If you can't . . . a slave." Webb and Nelson, 6.

p. 4. "hateful policemen." S. Rubin, 1.

p. 4. "Well, killing . . . Mississippi registered." Ibid.

p. 5. "The right . . . the community." NVRMI booklet *Children of the Movement*, 20.

p. 5. "Students did . . . skipped school." Ibid., 29–30.

p. 5. "Most of . . . the ballot." Ibid., 17.

p. 5. "We were . . . nonviolent way." NVRMI booklet *Student Foot Soldiers*.

p. 6. "I was eight . . . coming together." NVRMI booklet *Children of the Movement*, 16.

p. 6. "I'm going . . . of Congress." Berman, 16.

p. 6. "We must . . . the thousands." Partridge, 7.

p. 6. "Don't worry . . . all mankind." Ibid., 9.

p. 7. NEVER. Berman, 17.

p. 7. "Negroes . . . overcome us." Webb and Nelson, 69.

p. 7. "Although I . . . to vote here." NVRMI booklet *Children of the Movement*, 42.

p. 8. "I gotta keep on." Webb and Nelson, 60.

p. 8. "There are . . . voting rolls." Berman, 21.

p. 8. "When we . . . one toilet." NVRMI booklet *Children of the Movement*, 17.

p. 8. "I spent . . . concrete floor." Ibid., 28.

p. 9. "We took . . . jailers awake." Ibid., 19.

p. 9. "Two months . . . my life." Ibid., 26.

p. 9. "hadn't even . . . a chance." Webb and Nelson, 6.

p. 9. "hold . . . could vote." Ibid., 72.

CHAPTER 2

p. 10. "Give us . . . the ballot." Partridge, 7.

p. 11. "Jimmie Jackson . . . in vain." Berman, 4.

p. 11. "Walk for Freedom." Ibid., 21.

p. 11. "The police . . . my body." NVRMI booklet *Children of the Movement*, 42.

p. 12. "Tear gas!" Berman, 22.

p. 12. "The tear . . . not see." NVRMI booklet *Children of the Movement*, 16.

p. 13. "The march is legitimate." Berman, 23.

p. 13. "Turn Around Tuesday." Partridge, 34.

p. 14. "Every American . . . shall . . . overcome." Berman, 27–28.

p. 14. "We will . . . be passed." Berman, 29.

p. 16. "That's quite a crowd." Ibid., 31.

p. 16. "I'm here . . . I'm here!" Lowery, 101.

p. 17. "They told . . . us around." Berman, 32.

CHAPTER 3

p. 18. "Nobody's free . . . everybody's free." Hamer, 136.

p. 19. "It didn't . . . first place." Berman, 42.

p. 19. "Chris, you . . . [literacy] test." Ibid., 44.

p. 19. "Would you . . . would come." Ibid.

p. 20. "It was . . . Deep South." Ibid., 43.

p. 20. "I just . . . [made it here]." Ibid., 50.

p. 20. "Man, this . . . this time." Ibid., 51.

p. 20. "I'm going . . . LONG time." Ibid.

p. 20. "Although I . . . vote, counts." NVRMI booklet *Student Foot Soldiers*.

CHAPTER 4

p. 21. "I agree . . . for us." Stewart, 239.

p. 21. "in the . . . it happened." Miranda, Lin-Manuel, *Hamilton*.

p. 22. "Twenty years!" Stewart, 157.

p. 22. "high crimes and misdemeanors." Ibid., 215.

p. 23. "make enemies." Ibid., 185.

p. 23. "by the people." Ibid., 204.

p. 23. "We the . . . *United States*." Ibid., 234.

p. 24. "errors . . . for us." Ibid., 239.

CHAPTER 5

p. 26. "A voteless . . . hopeless people." Partridge, 2.

p. 26. "wiser or better." Keyssar, 30.

p. 26. "The mass . . . self-government." Ibid., 35.

p. 29. "hollow . . . man." May, x.

p. 29. "race war." Blight. *New York Times* article.

p. 29. "Slavery is not . . . has the ballot." Ibid.

p. 29. "of race . . . of servitude." May, xi.

p. 30. "The plan . . . white people." Ibid., xii.

p. 31. "It was . . . hopeless people." Partridge, 2.

CHAPTER 6

p. 32. "I labor . . . and sex." Terrell, 470.

p. 32. "Remember the . . . or Representation." Holton, 99–100.

p. 32. "stimulated" . . . "new Priviledges." Ibid., 102.

p. 33. "Sambos." Staples, *New York Times* article.

p. 34. "Whatever rights . . . the polls." Keyssar, 152.

p. 34. "cut off . . . the woman." Conkling, 89.

p. 34. "You must . . . the pen." Bausum, 23.

p. 34. "When he . . . want to vote." Ibid.

p. 35. "the family . . . everlasting quarrels." Keyssar, 155.

p. 35. "rough and tumble . . . worst" Ibid., 154.

p. 36. "Women are . . . worn-out traditions." Bausum, 33.

p. 38. "I labor . . . and sex." Terrell, 470.

p. 39. "If the . . . are lost." Conkling, 197.

p. 40. WE DEMAND . . . THE COUNTRY. Ibid., 201.

p. 40. "There would . . . at home." Ibid., 202.

p. 40. "Yesterday the . . . howling mob." Ibid., 204.

p. 40. "This mistreatment . . . to us." Ibid.

CHAPTER 7

p. 42. "I should be proud . . . American women." Conkling, 216.

p. 42. "I have . . . your administration." Bausum, 35.

p. 42. HOW LONG . . . WOMAN SUFFRAGE? Conkling, 215.

p. 42. "promote the welfare." R. Rubin, *Oberlin Alumni Magazine* article, 30.

p. 43. "swell . . . from freezing." Terrell, 355.

p. 43. "Silent Sentinels." Conkling, 216.

p. 43. "grand picket." Bausum, 40.

p. 44. "The world . . . for democracy." Ibid., 41.

p. 44. "We have . . . own government." McCarter, 198.

p. 44. "unwomanly . . . unpatriotic." Bausum, 42.

p. 44. "causing a . . . obstructing traffic." Ibid., 42–43.

p. 45. "jailbirds." Ibid., 51.

p. 45. "Dear Mother . . . delightful rest." Ibid., 47.

p. 45. "I went . . . the door." Stevens, 113.

p. 45. "We determined . . . in jail." Ibid., 113.

p. 45. "Yesterday was . . . is horrible." Conkling, 244.

p. 46. "All the . . . this again." Stevens, 119.

CHAPTER 8

p. 47. "Night of terror." Conkling, 248; Stevens, 129.

p. 47. "A man . . . outside the cell." Stevens, 123.

p. 47. "break the . . . white ladies." McCarter, 196.

p. 47. "We thought . . . my bed." Stevens, 123.

p. 47. "night of terror." Ibid., 129.

p. 48. "unknown tortures going on." Ibid., 124.

p. 48. "Operation leaves . . . ball of lead." Ibid., 125.

p. 48. "Still others . . . 'night of terror.' " Ibid., 129.

p. 49. "obstructing sidewalk traffic" Bausum, 59.

p. 51. "It was . . . for freedom." Stevens, 132.

CHAPTER 9

p. 52. "Hurrah . . . for Suffrage." East Tennessee Historical Society, online article.

p. 52. "We have . . . of women." Keyssar, 174.

p. 53. "Save a . . . the War." Cooper, Poster from Library of Congress.

p. 53. "Holding a . . . a statue." Stevens, 143.

p. 53. "The place . . . odors within." Ibid., 144.

p. 53. "The torch . . . without action." Bausum, 64.

p. 53. GREAT WAR . . . IS HERE. Library of Congress.

p. 54. "I have . . . here unwon." Bausum, 66.

p. 56. "to the last ditch, and then some." Conkling, 262.

p. 56. leaped off . . . to vote yes. Bausum, 79.

p. 56. "Hurrah . . . in doubt." East Tennessee Historical Society, online article.

p. 57. "Aye." Conkling, 264.

p. 57. "I knew . . . for ratification." Ibid., 264.

p. 57. "certificate of ratification." Bausum, 80.

p. 57. "We women . . . need it more." Terrell, 349.

p. 58. "Who has . . . decided today." Lowery, 121.

CHAPTER 10

p. 59. "Dead or . . . good vote." Campbell, 56.

p. 59. "freeholds." Ibid., 6.

p. 61. "party tickets," Lepore, *New Yorker* article.

p. 61. "ruffian . . . ordinary courage." Ibid.

p. 61. "a 'wrong vote.' " Campbell, 17.

p. 61. "I don't . . . New York City." Ibid., 62.

p. 61. "rowdies." Ibid., 20.

p. 63. "Observers . . . civic pride." Ibid.

p. 63. "pipe-layers." Ibid., 23.

p. 63. "regulate." Ibid., 48.

p. 63. "repeaters." Ibid., 23.

p. 63. "those . . . a right." Ibid., 23.

p. 63. "Dead or . . . good vote." Ibid., 56.

p. 63. "special constables." Ibid., 56.

p. 65. "forgotten minority." Berman, 105.

p. 66. "Chinese must go!" Freedman, *Angel Island*, 12.

CHAPTER 11

p. 67. "All elections . . . without it." Campbell, 123.

p. 67. "Beware! . . . the moonlight." Ibid., 59.

p. 67. "I am . . . twenty-four hours." Ibid., 60.

p. 67. "It has . . . strictly true." Ibid., 61.

p. 68. "uniform election . . . of voting." Ibid., 65.

p. 69. "repeaters." Ibid., 23.

p. 69. "When you've . . . four votes." Ibid., 86.

p. 69. "No honorable . . . honestly made." Ibid., 80.

p. 70. "If the . . . to himself." Ibid., 97.

p. 70. "It is . . . presents itself." Ibid., 100.

p. 70. "All elections . . . without it." Ibid., 123.

p. 70. "phantom." Ibid., 124.

p. 71. "Many of . . . civil courts." Ibid., 129.

p. 71. "free and fair." Ibid., 131.

p. 71. "triumph of democracy." Ibid., 132.

CHAPTER 12

p. 72. "One person, one vote." Campbell, 236.

p. 72. "The counting . . . to win." Ibid., 153.

p. 72. "I may . . . the last." O'Brien, 24.

p. 73. "I want . . . for war." Ibid., 35.

p. 73. "Miss Rankin . . . represents Montana." Woelfle, 50.

p. 73. "I believe . . . stop war." Ibid., 51.

p. 74. "culture of corruption." Campbell, 151.

p. 74. "Kingfish." Ibid., 198.

p. 74. "oversaw." Ibid., 203.

p. 75. "their actions . . . even fisticuffs." Ibid., 205.

p. 75. "The conception . . . one vote." Ibid., 236.

p. 76. "You haven't . . . twenty years." Ibid., 237

p. 76. "Mr. Carter . . . mad as hell." Ibid., 238.

p. 76. "My husband's . . . election year." Carter, 112.

p. 77. "fair and free." Ibid., xiv.

CHAPTER 13

p. 78. "Old enough . . . to vote." Keyssar, 225.

p. 78. "Fight at 18 . . . at 18." Key. *Atlanta Journal* article.

p. 78. "Old enough . . . to vote." Keyssar, 225.

p. 78. "If a . . . to vote." Ibid., 225.

p. 78. "To my . . . than reflection." Ibid., 226.

p. 80. "Young people . . . its history." Ibid.

p. 81. "Those who . . . political equality." Ibid., 227.

p. 82. "young Americans . . . moral strength." Ibid., 228.

CHAPTER 14

p. 83. "We're voting and we matter." Hernandez, interview with author.

p. 84. "It was very . . . we matter." Ibid.

p. 84. "Gore was . . . environmental change," A. Rubin, interview with author.

p. 85. "I voted . . . and trustworthy." Kolpas, interview with author.

p. 85. "I really . . . really started." Decker, *Los Angeles Times* article.

p. 85. "fake news" Osnos, Remmick, and Yaffa, *New Yorker* article.

p. 86. "It's hard . . . look dumb." Davis, interview with author.

p. 86. "President Trump . . . to accept." Peck, letter to the editor, *New York Times*.

p. 86. "I'm thrilled . . . court appointments." Robertson, letter to the editor, *New York Times*.

p. 87. "The fact . . . my community." Ford, WPIX broadcast.

p. 87. "I woke . . . state level." Haskell. Democratic Legislative Campaign Committee website.

p. 87. "We're going to change history." Yoon-Hendricks, *New York Times* article.

CHAPTER 15

p. 88. "At the . . . what is right." NVRMI booklet *Children of the Movement*, 58.

p. 88. "I still . . . for granted." White, interview with author.

p. 88. "Come back . . . voter's rights." S. Rubin, 73.

p. 89. "The VRA . . . an injustice!" White, interview with author.

p. 89. "The Supreme . . . Rights Act." Berman, *Rolling Stone* article.

p. 89. "Do you . . . has ended?" Whitaker, online article.

p. 90. "Things had changed dramatically." Rainey, online article.

p. 90. "Aborigines . . . in 2010." Sorkin, *New Yorker* article.

p. 91. "Congress Must . . . Act Promise." Austin-Hillery. Billmoyers.com blog.

p. 91. To Protect . . . Rights Act." Pérez and Zhou. *Christian Science Monitor* opinion piece.

p. 91. "Let America vote." Whitford, Let America Vote, online.

p. 91. "The right . . . right to vote." NVRMI booklet *Student Foot Soldiers*.

p. 91. "I was . . . of the struggle." *Student Foot Soldiers.*

Chapter 16

p. 93. "I feel . . . this state." Horwitz, *Washington Post* article.

p. 93. "Republicans are . . . from voting." Gearan and Chokshi, *Washington Post* article.

p. 93. "The intent . . . in this state." Horwitz, *Washington Post* article.

p. 94. "I don't . . . to vote." Berman, 260.

p. 94. "They want . . . years ago." Burch, *New York Times* article.

p. 95. "I don't . . . raking leaves." Koranda, online article.

p. 96. "John Test." Fund, online article.

p. 96. "I do . . . to vote." Minnite, 135.

CHAPTER 17

p. 97. "I've always . . . doesn't count." Whitford, online article.

p. 97. "horrid monster . . . The Gerry-Mander." *Boston Gazette*, March 26, 1812.

p. 97. "packed" . . . "cracked." Whitford, online article.

p. 99. "broken-winged . . . the state." *Baltimore Sun* editorial, March 8, 2018.

p. 100. "Democrats hate . . . do it." Lewis, online article.

CHAPTER 18

p. 101. "We want change!" Strauss, *Washington Post* article.

p. 101. "We may . . . can imagine." *New York Times* editorial, March 14, 2018.

p. 101. "By more . . . to happen." Dolasia, online article.

p. 101. "Adults have . . . that much." Saul and Hartocollis, *New York Times* article.

p. 101. "High schoolers . . . 18 to 16." Steinberg, *New York Times* article.

p. 102. "Too many . . . America's problems." Wang, *Washington Post* article.

p. 103. "Thirteen- to . . . is power!" NVRMI booklet *Story of the Voting Rights Struggle,* 28.

p. 103. "If you see . . . all about." Lewis, *Los Angeles Times* article.

PHOTO CREDITS

INDEX

Italic page numbers refer to illustrations.